D1506679

Miracles Happen!

JOAN HUNTER

BroadStreet
PUBLISHING

BroadStreet Publishing® Group, LLC
Savage, Minnesota, USA
BroadStreetPublishing.com

Miracles Happen!

Copyright © 2020 by Joan Hunter

978-1-4245-5950-3 (faux leather)
978-1-4245-5951-0 (e-book)

Stock or custom editions of BroadStreet Publishing titles may be purchased in bulk for educational, business, ministry, fundraising, or sales promotional use. For information, please email info@broadstreetpublishing.com.

Cover and interior by Garborg Design at GarborgDesign.com

I dedicate this book to Naida, whom I have known for over forty years. She served my parents for many years and helped them coordinate and edit their books.

She loves helping people get healed and set free through the written word. I am grateful for her passion for sharing the message of miracles and for helping me put the revelations that God gives me onto the page. Her love and devotion first to God, then to her family, and then to me and all he has called me to do, especially in books, speak volumes to her integrity.

Thank you so much for standing with me through good times and bad and helping me share the love of Jesus to those who read these pages. Finally, thank you for praying for me and for being a friend and coworker in the kingdom of God.

With much love and appreciation,

Joan

Contents

Introduction

Your choice to pick up this book was not an accident. Right now, God is directing your steps. He wants you to recognize the miracles in the world around you as well as those he wrote about in his Word. The Bible is full of miracles, but God's miracles don't stop there. They continue today. We just have to learn to see them. *Miracles Happen!* is designed to help you do just that.

This book is unique. It is different than other books I have written before, and I am so excited you have chosen to read it. These pages are filled with miracles that happened through the hands of Jesus and many others in the Bible as well as miracles that have occurred during my ministry and with other people I know. My hope is that these stories will raise your level of expectancy for God to do miracles in every area of your life.

I want to show you the many ways you can recognize God's miracles. I want the stories and miracles you read here to open your eyes to what God does around and through you every day. And, finally, I pray this book will totally transform the way you think about miracles.

Get ready to witness his daily miracles! God bless you as you read.

Pray this prayer:

Father God, I am excited about the message you have for me within these pages. Open my eyes to see your miracles in my life. Thank you for loving me and for the miracle of my life. Amen.

1

A God of Miracles

Miracles surround us every day. God's creation is filled with marvelous things that cannot be explained by human understanding. These events are often called *supernatural*, and you may wonder what that even means. *What is the supernatural? And is there a secret to things being supernatural?*

Listening to the world's explanation of a supernatural God and his Bible can get confusing. You may hear such terms as *weird, eerie,* or *bizarre,* but God's miracles are nothing like that. What God does is wonderful, amazing, awesome, and indeed, supernatural.

Only God's Spirit can open your eyes to seeing and understanding what he is doing in his world today. Some people believe God stopped creating after the first account of creation as described in the book of Genesis, but if God is the same forever, why would he stop creating after those first few days? He spoke, and the world appeared. His words created things supernaturally. Read Genesis. It is a book of miracles from beginning to end. And God continues even today to write his authority on everything we see, feel, or hear.

You may ask, "So did miracles start with the Bible?" No. They first started with creation, and the Bible documented them once the written word was developed. Truly the book of Genesis describes one miracle after another as God spoke the world into existence. This includes his creation of Adam and Eve. And God didn't stop there. Miracles are well documented throughout both the Old Testament and the New Testament.

Your next question might be, "Did miracles stop with the Bible?" Again my answer would be no! Thousands of books have been written over the centuries, telling of how the Lord has worked through his people, and all those events are truly miraculous. I believe God uses us to do his miracle work on earth today. The Bible says God even gives his people ideas for witty inventions and developments. (See Proverbs 8:12 KJV.)

- It is God who works in you both to will and to do for His good pleasure. (Philippians 2:13 NKJV)

- He who supplies the Spirit to you and works miracles among you, does He do it by the works of the law, or by the hearing of faith? (Galatians 3:5 NKJV)

- There are many ways in which God works in our lives, but it is the same God who does the work in and through all of us who are his. (1 Corinthians 12:6 TLB)

We only need to watch for the ways he works in our lives today to know this is true. His Word did not stop with the Bible, and it does not stay silent. It continues onward forever through us!

So, what is a miracle? The *Microsoft Encarta Dictionary* defines a miracle as "an event that appears to be contrary to the laws of nature and is regarded as an act of God, something admired as a marvelous creation or example of a particular type of science or skill or an event or action that is amazing, extraordinary, or unexpected." The *Microsoft Encarta Thesaurus* adds: "A wonder, marvel, sensation, vision, dream." I would dare to add that a miracle is an unexplainable occurrence which would seem impossible without God's assistance, intervention, or plan.

Miracles don't just happen out of the blue. If you understand that God is watching over you and protecting you during your short time on earth, you can rest in the fact that he has assigned his angels to protect you and arrange what you need to learn and do along your journey. Accepting Jesus as Lord and welcoming his Spirit to live within you assures you of his guidance and wisdom whenever you call upon him. He is there to help you navigate every hour of every day. Once you understand why miracles are important to your walk with him, you will begin to recognize when those miracles manifest themselves right in front of you.

So why are miracles necessary?

Because God loves you! You are his child, and God has a specific purpose for your life. You are a miracle.

Each life is a miracle. Truly, every part of creation is a miracle. Nothing just happens. Everything in life has a reason and purpose, and everything is connected to the almighty God—the God who leads and guides you.

He may often surprise his children with miracles that they don't readily recognize. But once your eyes are open to his handiwork, you can see miracles all around you. You can see that he is the same God today as he was at creation. And when you recognize God's miracles in your everyday life, you can respond with your praise, worship, and thanksgiving. He certainly is awesome in his power, authority, and creativity. And God totally deserves your grateful appreciation of his numerous blessings every day. Keep in mind, every breath you take is a gift, a miracle from God.

Pray this prayer:

Let me see your marvelous works, Father. Let me recognize the miracles in my life. And I will give you the praise. In Jesus's name. Amen.

2

Miracles Glorify God

God, the Creator of all things, is forever and ever in control of all things. He is in charge! He is almighty, omnipotent, omnipresent, and wonderful—truly, the ultimate Father. Nothing is impossible for God. His Word tells us very plainly what he can do, what he will do, and what he has already done for you and for me. And all he has done and will do glorifies him and his Son. With every miracle you read about, experience, or see, you can and should give God all the glory and thanksgiving you can muster. Allow your faith to grow and develop as you realize all miracles are from him. Each supernatural manifestation should increase your faith, belief, and love for your Father in heaven. God blesses you daily by surrounding you with his miraculous plans for every step you take.

I am often asked questions like "Does God heal this?" or "Can he heal that?" Too often, people limit God. There is nothing too hard for him. Not only can God heal any illness, but God can also replace an organ that has been removed. Read the following passages and take the limits off what God can do.

- "Behold, I am the LORD, the God of all flesh; is there anything too difficult for Me?" (Jeremiah 32:27 AMP)

- "I am the LORD, I do not change." (Malachi 3:6 NKJV)

- Jesus looked at them and said to them, "With men this is impossible, but with God all things are possible." (Matthew 19:26 NKJV)

While some people believe God can cure physical problems, they may not believe he can cure emotional or mental issues—things like PTSD, bipolar disorder, fibromyalgia, or schizophrenia. With man, there is no treatment, medication, or medical cure for these things. Medical science can often control the symptoms, but it can't cure these disorders or diseases. But God. Contrary to medical beliefs, I have seen many people healed of PTSD, bipolar disorder, fibromyalgia, and schizophrenia. Let's look at a few other verses that show God's glorious power straight from the mouth of his Son:

- Jesus came close to them and said, "All the authority of the universe has been given to me." (Matthew 28:18 TPT)

- Jesus said to him, "If you can believe, all things are possible to him who believes." (Mark 9:23 NKJV)

- Jesus replied, "The things that are impossible for people are possible for God." (Luke 18:27 ISV)

When people see God's miracles or experience his power, it opens their eyes. They realize God and Jesus are alive and love them very much. God does heal today just like he did in the Bible. Not only does he *want* to heal, but he also heals to glorify himself in the greatest way that there is. We saw this often throughout the Old Testament and especially in the New Testament with Jesus. Jesus's miracles were known by many—and not just by those who believed he was the Son of God.

- All the people were astounded as they saw with their own eyes the incredible miracle Jesus had performed! They began to say among themselves, "He really is the One— the true prophet we've been expecting!" (John 6:14 TPT)

- The Pharisees and the chief priests called a special meeting of the High Council and said, "So what are we going to do about this man? Look at all the great miracles he's performing!" (John 11:47 TPT)

Jesus's miracles were proof that he was indeed the Son of God—the true prophet Israel had been waiting for. And he wanted his miracle work to continue long after he was gone. So before Jesus died, he gave the gift of miracle healing to his disciples (and now to us). In Mark 16:17–18, Jesus said, "'And these signs will follow those who believe: In My name they will cast out demons; they will speak with new tongues; they will take up serpents; and if they drink anything deadly, it will by no means hurt them; they will lay hands on the sick, and they will recover'" (NKJV).

Did you know that God has commissioned us to perform miracles? It's true! And as we minister to the sick, other people will look to us and comment on the signs and wonders that follow us. Signs and wonders are scriptural. God's Word says in John 14:12, "'For sure, I tell you, whoever puts his trust in Me can do the things I am doing. He will do even greater things than these because I am going to the Father'" (NLV). Miracles happen as we lay hands on the sick and pray for them. God does these miracles through you, a believer. Just remember that God must get the credit and the glory for every miracle.

Stephen and Philip are two examples of men who took Jesus's words to heart and went on to perform miracles in his name and for his glory. Acts 6:8 says, "Stephen, who was a man full of grace and supernatural power, performed many astonishing signs and wonders and mighty miracles among the people" (TPT). This is a very important passage. Stephen was full of grace and supernatural power and did many mighty miracles among the people. How did he get full of grace and power? He studied the teachings of Jesus, learned from people around him, and acted on what he learned and saw. This same supernatural power will grow the more you study, learn, lay hands on people, and see them recover. Follow Stephen's example just as he followed what he learned from Jesus's disciples.

And then there's Philip, who also performed miracles. Acts 8:6 says, "And the multitudes with one accord heeded the things spoken by Philip, hearing and seeing the miracles which he did" (NKJV). People respected Philip and believed he was a man of God because of what they saw. He didn't have any special powers that weren't available to someone else. He simply believed that God could work through him, and he acted in obedience. Clearly, God can and does use ordinary people to do extraordinary things!

As people see God use you in a supernatural way, their faith will grow also. When the disciples and servants witnessed the miracles Jesus performed at the wedding, people believed: "Jesus performed this miracle, the first of His signs, in Cana of Galilee. They did not know how this happened; but when the disciples and the servants witnessed this miracle, their faith blossomed" (John 2:11 VOICE). Witnessing you laying hands on the sick and seeing them recover will show people God's power flowing through you. Witnessing miracles always astounds and changes people. It is an experience no one ever forgets.

After teaching and leading the audience in the sinner's prayer during a service, I always ask people to turn to a person next to them. I direct them to pray specifically for the other person's needs. Many times, it's for healing. And do you know what happens? Miraculous healings pop up all over the room. Someone doesn't have to be saved for years before praying for another person. Even a new believer can lay hands on the sick and see them recover. Because it isn't about us. It's about God working through us. This is often the first experience of healing a new believer sees and feels. And because of what they have witnessed, they can't help but give God the glory!

This happened often in the Bible. As people saw or heard about miracles being performed, their faith and belief grew.

- While Jesus was at the Passover Feast, the number of his followers began to grow, and many gave their allegiance to him because of all the miraculous signs they had seen him doing! (John 2:23 TPT)

- All the multitude kept silent and listened to Barnabas and Paul declaring how many miracles and wonders God had worked through them among the Gentiles. (Acts 15:12 NKJV)

Right now, get a pad of paper and a pen. Jot down the miracles in your life that come to mind and continue doing so as you read this book. Thank God for each one. When you need encouragement, pull out your list to remind yourself of what he has already done and promises to do for you today and tomorrow. He is certainly well-qualified to bless you with supernatural miracles. Give him all the glory, praise, and thanksgiving. Your response shows him you trust him and agree with what he is doing. There is power in agreement. And God wants you to give him all the glory as miracles manifest in your life. Miracles truly glorify Jesus as well as his Father.

Finally, remember that as you go out to minister, you need people agreeing with you. Matthew 18:19 says, "Again, truly I tell you that if two of you on earth agree about anything they ask for, it will be done for them by my Father in heaven" (NIV). This verse shows the power of a partner or prayer partner. This person doesn't necessarily need to be in the same room with you while you pray because prayers travel any distance instantly. Remember, don't limit God! The important thing is the *agreement* of those who are praying.

Unity and acting in total agreement will increase the expression of God's power and the miraculous healings that will happen through the prayers of believers. On the other hand, controversy and dissension hinder God's power to flow through human hands. I have full confidence that my ministry prayer partners are praying for me regardless of where I happen to be in the world. Those prayers increase the power of my prayers when ministering to the sick. And God's blessings flow back to those who are praying as well.

Pray this prayer:

Father, I know you are doing great things in my life, and I know you can do great things through me. I choose to walk in agreement with you and with others who are doing your work. In Jesus's name. Amen.

3

Miracle of Protection

How many of us fall to our knees and cry out for God when we are facing a serious challenge? This is quite common when we are afraid and need protection for ourselves or our families. It could be an illness, a job loss, or a child who has gone astray. No matter the reason, we recognize our desperate need for our Father in these situations. Our human wisdom is exhausted, and we don't know what to do next to solve the problem. But God. He is always waiting for us and ready to help. He is there to protect us.

The Israelites and the Miracle of Protection

Imagine being in bondage in Egypt for hundreds of years. During that time, God's people certainly bombarded him with prayers wanting to be free from Pharaoh's rule. I doubt anyone would argue that they didn't need a miracle or two. During each encounter with Pharaoh, Moses spoke, and plagues appeared from nowhere. Frogs, gnats, insects, boils, hail, locusts, death of livestock, water turned to blood, unusual darkness during the day and night, and the deaths of the firstborn children. You would think that Pharaoh would have been smart enough to free the Israelite slaves before the nation was so devastated. Clearly, God wasn't going to give up or run out of ideas. A supernatural God sent forth each of these plagues. And with every plague the Egyptians suffered while God shielded his people from harm. Talk about supernatural miracles! Talk about the miracle of protection!

And God's miracles didn't stop with the plagues. One of the most vivid scenes of God's protection of the Israelites took place during their exodus from Egypt. Pharaoh's permission to allow the hundreds of thousands of Israelite slaves to go free after 430 years of bondage was a miracle in itself. But as soon as the Israelites were gone, Pharaoh and his army followed in hot pursuit! When Moses and the Israelites came to the Red Sea, they found a seemingly impossible barrier to their escape. But God. He told Moses to stretch out his rod over the sea. When he did, God pushed the sea aside so the Israelites could cross. Can you imagine the mud and debris that is normally at the bottom of a wide body of water? God even dried the riverbed and removed any other barriers so the fleeing masses could reach safety on the other side (Exodus 14:16, 28–30).

In this story, people often place emphasis on the parting of the waters. Some say the water was only a few inches deep. But I have a question. What was the bigger miracle? The parting of the sea or what came next? When Pharaoh's army tried to cross the parted sea in pursuit of the Israelites, God ordered Moses to again stretch out his hand over the sea. When he did, God made the water close over the Egyptians, not leaving a single survivor. Israel saw the dead bodies of Pharaoh's army (along with their horses and chariots) washed ashore. Do you think if the sea contained only a few inches of water it would have destroyed all those men, horses, and chariots?

God protected his children from destruction. He conquered the enemy without a sword or shield, using just his power and his love. The entire book of Exodus is full of one miracle after another—from the burning bush to the plagues to the crossing of the Red Sea. During the entire forty years of wandering in the desert, God's miracle of protection surrounded his children, and he supplied for their every need.

Protection for Daniel

Do you remember the story of Daniel and the lions' den? God calmed the lions so they wouldn't attack and destroy Daniel when the king threw him into the pit for their next meal. The carnivorous animals were hungry and waiting for a nice snack. Did God hide Daniel from their sharp eyes or camouflage the human smell? Whatever happened, Daniel was safe and very much alive the next morning. This miracle showed God's protection over Daniel's life. Daniel 6:27 says of our God of protection, "He delivers and rescues, and He works signs and wonders in heaven and on earth, who has delivered Daniel from the power of the lions" (NKJV).

Protection from Scorpions and Snakes

Throughout the Bible, God reveals his miracle of protection in story after story, even with scorpions and serpents:

- "I have given you authority over all the power of the Enemy, and to walk among serpents and scorpions and to crush them. Nothing shall injure you!" (Luke 10:19 TLB)

- When Paul had gathered a bundle of sticks and laid them on the fire, a viper came out because of the heat, and fastened on his hand. So when the natives saw the creature hanging from his hand, they said to one another, "No doubt this man is a murderer, whom, though he has escaped the sea, yet justice does not allow to live." But he shook off the creature into the fire and suffered no harm. However, they were expecting that he would swell up or suddenly fall down dead. But after they had looked for a long time and saw no harm come to

him, they changed their minds and said
that he was a god. (Acts 28:3–6 NKJV)

I certainly don't advocate picking up poisonous
snakes or trying any other dangerous stunt to show off
or try to force God; however, if the enemy suddenly
attacks, trying to distract or destroy you, you can be
confident that God's angels are nearby and will step in
the fray to protect you. God protected his disciples and
followers so that they could further spread the gospel,
and he will protect you. Remember, nothing is impossible for him!

Protection for All God's Children

But how can we be sure that God will protect us?
Because his Word promises this. If you love him and
believe in his Word, he is more than willing to take care
of you and your family.

- You who love the LORD, hate evil; He pro-
  tects the souls of His godly ones (believers), He rescues them from the hand of the
  wicked. (Psalm 97:10 AMP)

- The LORD will protect you from all evil; He will keep your life. (Psalm 121:7 AMP)

- "No weapon that is formed against you will succeed; and every tongue that rises against you in judgment you will condemn. This [peace, righteousness, security, and triumph over opposition] is the heritage of the servants of the LORD, and this is their vindication from Me," says the LORD. (Isaiah 54:17 AMP)

Think about times when you could have faced disaster. Then suddenly, there was a way of escape. That was God at work in your life. The same God who saved the Israelites and protected them from Pharaoh's army is working in your life today, protecting you from harm and from the enemy.

During my first trip to Haiti, there were many instances of demon manifestation in our services. Many people were demonically wiggling, and the ushers would bring them to the front altar and lay them at my feet. The first few times, I was a bit uneasy about this. These people were so overwhelmed by the power of God that they couldn't stand up. They just lay there on the ground for about thirty minutes. But when they finally did get up, they were completely healed. God had released the enemy from their bodies, and they were set free! Hallelujah!

Even before I left for Haiti that first time, I knew the witch doctors would try to stop my work there. When we finally arrived, they spit out their curses at me in an attempt to hurt me and stop the ministry to the people. But I never responded or reacted. I simply kept on doing what God had told me to do. I ministered to hurting people. Nothing bad ever happened to me. Interestingly enough, their curses went back onto them, making them fall helplessly to the floor. They were doing their best to hurt me, but their words of anger and hate returned to them. God's miracle of protection covers his people, keeping them safe and giving them the courage they need to continue to do his work.

Before I travel anywhere out of the country, such as any foreign trip to Haiti, Israel, or Europe, I always seed (give to God) $91.10 for supernatural miracle protection. And I truly believe that because of my act of faith, I have never been hurt or become sick during my travels around the world. My God protects me wherever he sends me because I am one of his favorites. He guides my steps. (See more information on seed offerings in my book *Supernatural Provision* where I explain scriptural giving.) Read these verses from Psalm 91 and Proverbs 2 and claim them over yourself and your loved ones:

- When we live our lives within the shadow
  of God Most High, our secret hiding place,
  we will always be shielded from harm.
  How then could evil prevail against us or
  disease infect us? (Psalm 91:9–10 TPT)

- The Lord has a hidden storehouse of wisdom made accessible to his godly lovers.
  He becomes your personal bodyguard
  as you follow his ways, protecting and
  guarding you as you choose what is right.
  (Proverbs 2:8 TPT)

- Keep me [in Your affectionate care, protect
  me] as the apple of Your eye; Hide me in
  the [protective] shadow of Your wings.
  (Psalm 17:8 AMP)

If you are in need of God's protection today, boldly ask him. And thank God for the protection he has already given.

Pray this prayer:

Father, I need your hand of protection every day. I don't see any plagues around me, but I know there are many invisible attacks from the enemy that could destroy me. Thank you for your hand of protection, Father. Thank you, in Jesus's name. Amen.

4

Miracle of Salvation

The next miracle that comes into play is that of salvation. Being born again by allowing Jesus to live within you sounds like a true miracle to me. All you have to do is believe in Jesus and accept his sacrifice and redemption given to us, just because he loves us . . . sinners though we are. What a miracle it is to move from darkness to light and anticipate a future in heaven instead of hell!

But receiving God's gift of salvation and being born again is really that simple. You can't earn it; you can't buy it. You just have to listen and believe. God has loved you since before you were a dot in your mother's womb. His love never changes, which means he still loves you today no matter what you have done before. And despite your sin, he still calls you to himself. God still wants a relationship with you. This is why salvation is often the first true miracle a person acknowledges.

Some people come into our services feeling hopeless and lost. Then, when they receive Jesus and the Holy Spirit, they walk out healed and whole. This was the case with a lady who was invited to one of my mom and dad's services many years ago. She had planned on committing suicide that night. Instead, she not only accepted Jesus, but she also received the baptism in the Holy Spirit and was healed. Needless to say, she did not end her life that night. No, God gave her a new life in him! She personally experienced God's miracle power of salvation.

If you are longing for this kind of redemption story, God's Word promises salvation if you just call on his name and ask him. Read these verses about the miracle of salvation:

- "'It shall come to pass that whoever calls on the name of the LORD shall be saved.'

Men of Israel, hear these words: Jesus of Nazareth, a Man attested by God to you by miracles, wonders, and signs which God did through Him in your midst, as you yourselves also know."
(Acts 2:21–23 NKJV)

- The same came to Jesus by night, and said unto him, Rabbi, we know that thou art a teacher come from God: for no man can do these miracles that thou doest, except God be with him. Jesus answered and said unto him, Verily, verily, I say unto thee, except a man be born again, he cannot see the kingdom of God. (John 3:2–3 KJV)

After reading these verses, if you want to receive the miracle of salvation, pray this simple prayer:

Father, it's me. You know all the things I have done. I have messed up a lot of things in the past. Please forgive me. Come into my heart and change my life. I want to live for you from this moment on. Guide me and teach me your ways. In Jesus's name. Amen.

By praying that prayer and meaning it, a miracle just happened! God just changed your destiny! You are now saved and on your way to heaven. Hallelujah! You can now open your eyes and heart to more of his miracles. Being saved with Jesus in your heart will help you better understand the rest of this book. Take notes. Write them in the margins of this book even. Have a Bible nearby and learn to confirm the miracles of God for yourself.

5

Miracle of Holy Spirit Baptism

After salvation, the next step is allowing Jesus to baptize you in the Holy Spirit. In God's Word, he promises to do many miracles through those who have the gift of his Spirit:

> "It shall come to pass in the last days,
> says God, that I will pour out of My

Spirit on all flesh; your sons and your daughters shall prophesy, your young men shall see visions, your old men shall dream dreams. And on My menservants and on My maidservants I will pour out My Spirit in those days; and they shall prophesy. I will show wonders in heaven above and signs in the earth beneath." (Acts 2:17–19 NKJV)

When you are baptized in the Holy Spirit, the supernatural will flow through you to others in many exciting ways. So keep your heart and eyes open as you read through the next section. Trust God to anoint your life and work a great miracle in you.

One Body with Different Gifts

All believers in Jesus belong to his body; however, we are all blessed with different gifts and abilities which we use to help one another walk, talk, and act more like Jesus along our path. Read God's Word and learn. Then discover the special gifts and talents God has blessed you with. For instance, remember the lady who wanted to commit suicide and instead got the Holy Spirit? She is now committed to praying for the sick and seeing them recover.

In my own life, the Holy Spirit baptism with speaking in tongues made a huge difference. Before the Holy Spirit, the sick occasionally got healed, but once I received the power of the baptism, people actually recovered their health while I prayed. Thousands have been healed over the years, and the miracles continue with every prayer I pray for those in need of God's healing. These healings include body, mind, soul, spirit, and finances. I document many of these testimonies throughout my books.

The Many Gifts of God

God miraculously gives many gifts and anointings to his children. Some are present most of the time. Other gifts manifest only when needed. God's Word clearly shows that God gives gifts and abilities to his children:

- God added his witness to theirs. He validated their ministry with signs, astonishing wonders, all kinds of powerful miracles, and by the gifts of the Holy Spirit, which he distributed as he desired. (Hebrews 2:4 TPT)

- You are the body of the Anointed One, and each of you is a unique and vital part of it. God has placed in the church the following: first apostles, second prophets, third teachers, then those with gifts of miracles, gifts of divine healing, gifts of revelation knowledge, gifts of leadership, and gifts of different kinds of tongues. Not everyone is an apostle or a prophet or a teacher. Not everyone performs miracles. (1 Corinthians 12:27–29 TPT)

- I ask you again, does God give you the power of the Holy Spirit and work miracles among you as a result of your trying to obey the Jewish laws? No, of course not. It is when you believe in Christ and fully trust him. (Galatians 3:5 TLB)

- "If you then, being evil, know how to give good gifts to your children, how much more will your heavenly Father give the Holy Spirit to those who ask Him!" (Luke 11:13 NKJV)

- God always has shown us that these messages are true by signs and wonders and various miracles and by giving certain special abilities from the Holy Spirit to those who believe; yes, God has assigned such gifts to each of us. (Hebrews 2:4 TLB)

- There are many ways in which God works in our lives, but it is the same God who does the work in and through all of us who are his. The Holy Spirit displays God's power through each of us as a means of helping the entire church. To one person the Spirit gives the ability to give wise advice; someone else may be especially good at studying and teaching, and this is his gift from the same Spirit. He gives special faith to another, and to someone else the power to heal the sick. He gives power for doing miracles to some, and to others power to prophesy and preach. He gives someone else the power to know whether evil spirits are speaking through those who claim to be giving God's messages—or whether it is really the Spirit of God who is speaking. Still another person is able to speak in languages he never learned; and others, who do not know the language either, are given power to understand what he is saying. It is the same and only Holy Spirit who gives all these gifts and powers, deciding which each one of us should have. (1 Corinthians 12:6–11 TLB)

God is a gift giver! He has given each of us unique gifts to share with the world. Some people are called natural born teachers. Guess what? That gift of teaching is from God. Some are excellent speakers. Some are doctors with the gift of healing while others may be writers, musicians, praise leaders, legislators, organizers, farmers, firemen—the list is endless. God blesses each person with what they need to fit into his family plan exactly when the gift is needed. It's time to discover what gifts he has blessed you with.

As you read the verses above, did any particular gift or ability pop out at you? If not, pray and ask God what gifts he has given you. Ask him to reveal those to you. And thank him for his many gifts and for the ability to use them to help others and to grow his kingdom. Most people baptized in the Holy Spirit actually have more than one of the gifts to use as God directs.

Speaking in Tongues

Can you speak another language which you have never studied or learned before? No, of course not. Most people speak only the native language they learned as a child. But prepare yourself for another miracle. This manifestation is called speaking in tongues and usually occurs following the baptism in the Holy Spirit. Luke speaks of this in Acts 2:2–4: "And suddenly there came a sound from heaven, as of a rushing mighty wind, and it filled the whole house where they were sitting. Then there appeared to them divided tongues, as of fire, and one sat upon each of them. And they were all filled with the Holy Spirit and began to speak with other tongues, as the Spirit gave them utterance" (NKJV).

Speaking in tongues is truly a sign and a wonder because you are speaking a language that you don't know or understand. It may sound like gibberish to you; however, you are actually speaking to God in a very special prayer language. Occasionally, someone nearby may understand exactly what you are saying in tongues. The message could be meant specifically for them from God. I call this a miracle. Speaking in tongues is truly a miracle. It bypasses your mind when you pray. If a specific person comes into your thoughts, he or she may need prayer. You don't need all the details. Just pray in the Spirit. The Holy Spirit will give you the specific words necessary as God intends. Trust him.

Another form of worship—and one of the most beautiful—is to *sing* in tongues. People who are tone deaf and can't sing at all can suddenly have an amazing glorious voice with perfect pitch and harmony when they sing in tongues. If you ever get to witness an experience like this, you will never forget it. My dad, Charles Hunter, had this marvelous gift. If you stood near him while singing a praise or worship song, you could hear him easily. He was worshipping with all his heart in another key. However, when everyone switched to singing in tongues, he was right on point singing a gorgeous melody or perfect harmony. I was inspired every time I heard him worship in tongues.

The Tower of Babel

The power of cooperation and common speech is shown in the story of Babel. The people were gaining so much power that God had to step in and do something. He confused their speech so that instead of communicating in one language, they spoke in several different languages. The people who could understand each other then divided into their own groups.

> The Lord said, "Indeed the people are one and they all have one language, and this is what they begin to do; now nothing that they propose to do will be withheld from them. Come, let Us go down and there confuse their language, that they may not understand one another's speech." So the LORD scattered them abroad from there over the face of all the earth, and they ceased building the city. Therefore its name is called Babel, because there the LORD confused the language of all the earth; and from there the LORD

scattered them abroad over the face of
all the earth. (Genesis 11:5–9 NKJV)

Imagine, chatting with new friends in your native language when, suddenly, you can no longer understand each other's words. You wouldn't be able to hang around those people for long. You have to find people who understand you and who you understand. And this is exactly how God worked in the story of the tower of Babel. By dividing the people and their languages, God halted the building of the tower and caused the people to spread over the earth, which was what he had asked them to do in the first place. This shows that God can and will do anything—even the seemingly impossible—to fulfill his will and purposes.

God and You

My parents, Charles and Frances Hunter, had been traveling and ministering for several years after they were married. They had heard many negative teachings about the Holy Spirit baptism and avoided that subject. They loved to pray for the sick and had a bit of success seeing every service and every prayer, more and more people were healed miraculously. Mom and Dad often would simply wave their hands over a large congregation. Those who had been sick would come forward to the front to give their testimonies of miraculous healing. My office still receives testimonies of people who were healed under Mom and Dad's ministry ten to twenty years ago. My parents traveled around the world to minister to the sick and saw them recover just as the Bible says: "And the apostles went out announcing the good news everywhere, as the Lord himself consistently worked with them, validating the message they preached with miracle-signs that accompanied them!" (Mark 16:20 TPT).

My dad would ask for one or two people who needed healing to follow him across the stage during a meeting. Then he would ask them where their problem or pain was. They would smile and say, "I'm healed. The pain is gone!" Dad would get a big grin on his face and reply, "Miracles follow me. You are a miracle."

Personally, I have continued my parents' ministry to do the same around the world. Miracles happen all the time wherever I go. My parents went on to teach others how to minister healing. I continue to do the same. Read my books. Listen to my videos. Attend my services and classes. Many are live streamed online and on YouTube. Check out my TV show *Miracles Happen!*

Am I sure all these blessings and gifts, not to mention miracles, will be evident in your life? Oh, yes, I am! His Word tells us miracles of all kinds will follow us. Open your heart and learn what God wants to do for you and through you. Exciting days are ahead for you!

Pray this prayer:

Father, I desire the baptism in your Holy Spirit just like the believers received on the day of Pentecost in the Bible. I want to talk to you in that special language only you will understand. I need the edification and encouragement praying in tongues will bring to my soul and spirit. I accept any and all special giftings you choose to give me to fulfill your call on my life. I am more than ready to

language and understanding. I want all your special gifts that come with the baptism of the Holy Spirit so I can minister your miracles to others in need. Bless me, Lord, with all you want to do for me. Thank you, Lord. In Jesus's name. Amen.

6

Miracle of Provision

Old Testament Provisions

If you go back to the Old Testament, you can see how God supplied his people with meat, fruit, and vegetables to survive. His children not only survived, but they also thrived and spread around the earth. One evidence of provision happened when Hezekiah reformed Israel by destroying all of the idols and bringing the people back under God's purpose and plan for them: "Azariah, chief priest of the family of Zadok, answered, 'From the moment of this huge outpouring of gifts to The Temple of GOD, there has been plenty to eat for everyone with food left over. GOD has blessed his people—just look at the evidence!'" (2 Chronicles 31:10 MSG)

Also, when you read the story of Joseph in the Old Testament, you can see how God moved Joseph and his family into Egypt to prevent them from starving during the famine. As the story begins, jealousy and hate rear their ugly heads. But God. He had a plan. He used these strained family relationships to save the Israelite nation. God gave Joseph wisdom to survive and prosper. He was even promoted and was able to minimize the famine's effects on Egypt and the surrounding area. Joseph's story had a happy and unexpected ending.

Years later when Joseph was gone, the Israelites multiplied and became enslaved by the Egyptians. But

Pharaoh's rule. Following the Israelites captivity in Egypt,

God came through with plenty of food for the next forty years as they wandered around the mountain. Time and time again he provided food for them, even when they grumbled and complained:

- "I have heard the grumbling of the Isra- elites. Tell them, 'At twilight you will eat meat, and in the morning you will be filled with bread. Then you will know that I am the LORD your God.'" That evening quail came and covered the camp, and in the morning there was a layer of dew around the camp. When the dew was gone, thin flakes like frost on the ground appeared on the desert floor. When the Israelites saw it, they said to each other, "What is it?" For they did not know what it was. Moses said to them, "It is the bread the LORD has given you to eat." (Exodus 16:12–15 NIV)

- "Tell the people: 'Consecrate yourselves in preparation for tomorrow, when you will eat meat. The LORD heard you when you wailed, "If only we had meat to eat! We

were better off in Egypt!" Now the LORD will give you meat, and you will eat it. You will not eat it for just one day, or two days, or five, ten or twenty days, but for a whole month—until it comes out of your nostrils and you loathe it—because you have rejected the LORD, who is among you, and have wailed before him, saying, "Why did we ever leave Egypt?"'"
(Numbers 11:18–20 NIV)

- He gave a command to the skies above and opened the doors of the heavens; he rained down manna for the people to eat, he gave them the grain of heaven. Human beings ate the bread of angels; he sent them all the food they could eat. He let loose the east wind from the heavens and by his power made

on them like dust, birds like sand on the seashore. He made them come down inside

till they were gorged—he had given them what they craved. (Psalm 78:23–29 NIV)

A variety of diet was missing, but God's mighty hand maintained their survival. Can you even imagine feeding thousands of people three meals a day for forty years and keeping their clothes from wearing out? This was truly miracle after miracle!

God's Provision for Elijah and Elisha

In addition to the Israelites, Elijah and Elisha also experienced God's bountiful blessings. Again and again, God provided for them in their time of need.

For Elijah, God even sent ravens to feed him in 1 Kings 17:1–6 until God sent him on to visit the widow in Zarephath. When he arrived at the widow's house, she and her son were starving from the famine. They had only a little flour and oil to make bread, which they planned to do and then die. But Elijah knew his God was bigger than that. So Elijah said to her:

> "Don't be afraid! Go ahead and cook that 'last meal,' but bake me a little loaf of bread first; and afterwards there will still be enough food for you and your son. For the Lord God of Israel

says that there will always be plenty of flour and oil left in your containers until the time when the Lord sends rain and the crops grow again!"

So she did as Elijah said, and she, Elijah, and her son continued to eat from her supply of flour and oil as long as it was needed. For no matter how much they used, there was always plenty left in the containers, just as the Lord had promised through Elijah. (1 Kings 17:13–16 TLB)

Elisha also experienced God's goodness during a famine in Gilgal:

Now [at another time] a man from Baal-shalisha came and brought the man of God bread of the first fruits, twent̶... of grain [in the husk] in his sack. And Elisha said, "Give it to th̶... [afte̶... may eat." His servant said, "How am

I to set [only] this before a hundred [hungry] men?" He said, "Give it to the people so that they may eat, for thus says the Lord, 'They shall eat and have some left.'" So he set it before them, and they ate and left some, in accordance with the word of the Lord.
(2 Kings 4:42–44 AMP)

These stories show that God's miracle of provision is evident in both big and small ways. He is just as concerned about providing for a widow and her son as he is in providing for one hundred hungry men. What a wonder this must have been for the people who witnessed these miracles! And how their faith in God must have grown!

New Testament Provisions

As you just read, the miracle of multiplication started many years before Jesus was born. However, the most common story we hear about is found in the New Testament when Jesus feeds the five thousand on a hillside.

The Feeding of Five Thousand

Can you even imagine being faced with feeding five thousand unexpected guests with only five loaves of bread and two fish in your kitchen? Four Gospel writers document this miraculous event (see Matthew 14:13–21, Mark 6:30–44, Luke 9:10–17, John 6:1–14 for the full accounts). Let's look at Mark's account: "Then Jesus took the five loaves and two fish, gazed into heaven, and gave thanks to God. He broke the bread and the two fish and distributed them to his disciples to serve the people—and the food was multiplied in front of their eyes! Everyone had plenty to eat and was fully satisfied. Then the twelve disciples picked up what remained, and each of them ended up with a basket full of leftovers!" (Mark 6: 41–43 TPT)

Try to imagine what it must have been like to be part of that crowd. To see one boy's lunch become food for five thousand hungry men, plus women and children? Many of the people in the crowd may not have even realized that a miracle was happening before their eyes. They were just thankful to have food to fill their bellies. But the miracle wouldn't have been lost on the disciples. Their eyes must have been wide as they watched those five loaves and two fish feed a hillside of people. Oh, how their faith must have grown that day!

The Feeding of Four Thousand

Not long after that banquet, Jesus did it again. This time, he fed four thousand people (see Matthew 15:32–39 and Mark 8:1–9). Again, let's look at Mark's account:

Jesus instructed the crowd to sit down on the grass. After he took the seven loaves, he gave thanks to God, broke them, and started handing them to his disciples. They kept distributing the bread until they had served the entire crowd. They also had a few small fish, and after giving thanks for these, Jesus had his disciples serve them to the crowd. Everyone ate until they were satisfied. Then the disciples gathered up the broken pieces and filled seven large baskets with the leftovers. About four thousand people ate the food that had been multiplied! (Mark 8:6–9 TPT)

If you read both of these accounts closely, the miracle actually manifested when the food was in the hands of the disciples as they passed it through the crowd. How must the disciples have felt to be passing those baskets among the crowd but never coming up empty? They must have been scratching their heads! Every person was fed, but that's not all. After everyone had feasted, there were twelve large baskets of food left over in the first story and seven in the second. Talk about multiplication and blessings! They had so much that they even left extra food behind.

Miracles of Fish

One day as the disciples were fishing and not catching anything, Jesus gave them a simple order that surprised them all: "And He said to them, 'Cast the net on the right side of the boat, and you will find some.' So they cast, and now they were not able to draw it in because of the multitude of fish. . . . Simon Peter went up and dragged the net to land, full of large fish, one hundred and fifty-three; and although there were so many, the net was not broken" (John 21:6, 11 NKJV).

I know a lot of fishermen who would love to have Jesus in their boat while fishing. They would save many hours of casting, dangling bait, and rowing. The disciples must have been very discouraged while sitting in their boat, waiting and hoping for a few fish to find their way into their net. But they weren't having much success that day. But Jesus. He surprised them all by supplying more fish than what they needed. I can only imagine how the disciples must have jumped up and worked to pull in that net full of fish!

On another occasion, Jesus supplied money for taxes in a rather humorous manner. In Matthew 17:26–27, when a tax collector approached Peter asking if his master paid taxes, Peter went to Jesus to ask what he should do. Jesus told Peter: "Go to the lake and throw out your hook, and the first fish that rises up will have a coin in its mouth. It will be the exact amount you need to pay the temple tax for both of us" (TPT). Now I haven't tried fishing to pay my taxes, but I do firmly believe if God told me to look in the mouth of a fish for a treasure, I would find something very special. God certainly has a sense of humor, and although Peter was grateful to find the money to pay the taxes, he must have laughed at the way Jesus provided! God's miracles should never cease to amaze us no matter how big or small they are.

God's Provision Today

I am a firsthand witness of God's bountiful blessings. Years ago, I was a single mother of four very active daughters. In addition to our fish and dogs, I had many hungry mouths to feed. I was left with nothing in the year 2000. I didn't know what to do except to spend hours praying and believing in God. My accountant advised me to file bankruptcy and stop giving so much of my income to God. I knew that advice did not line up with the Word or will of God. I fired him and found a CPA who believed the Word, and I continued to tithe.

One day, I was praying all the way home. *God, I don't have enough food in the house to feed the girls*, I cried out to him. I was worried and didn't see how I was going to make it another day. When I reached home, bags of groceries filled the kitchen—so many that they all couldn't fit into the pantry, cupboards, or refrigerator. Then, I checked the mailbox to find a check from a friend. I called to thank the person, who told me, "We can cut back, but we cannot leave you and your children without food."

Numerous times after that, there would be a knock at the door. I would find friends standing on the porch laden with bags of food. We never went hungry. I could have been too proud and refused the food and donations; however, I knew God would use people to bless us. And I knew I needed to accept those blessings from God. Every time I turned around, God brought in more supplies for my family of five. I tell you this so that, if you are going through a time such as this, you can know God will provide for your family just as he did for mine. Do not be anxious or afraid! He knows your every need. Look to him as your ultimate source. He will use other people to bless you. He will give you favor. As Luke 6:38 says, "Give, and it shall be given unto you; good measure, pressed down, and shaken together, and running over, shall men give into your bosom. For with the same measure that ye mete withal it shall be measured to you again" (KJV).

God will provide! Man shall give into your bosom. Just continue to "give and it shall be given to you."

Testimonies of the Miracle of Provision

People write to me all the time telling me how God has provided for them. My team gets great joy out of reading these stories and testimonies of God's goodness and provision. Read these testimonies of people who have received a miracle of provision and know that God will do the same for you in your time of need.

- I'm excited to report that yesterday I received a debt cancellation notice of $1,800! I am so grateful to the Lord for hearing my prayer, for being able to sow a seed, and I believe he's not done yet! Thank you for all you're doing! Blessings, NC

- A man had an IRS bill of $75,000. He gave $111 in an offering at one of my services. Before he even left the building, he got notice that the IRS had cancelled his entire debt. Needless to say, he was a very happy camper.

- My husband was in the middle of a serious court case. We needed $5000 as a retainer to pay a lawyer to represent him. Our finances were already stretched because of his hospitalizations and disability. We sold and pawned everything of value. Next, came a garage sale which brought in a meager $200. Since that was not enough, we went to church and gave the entire $200 and prayed for a miracle. Two days later, we were driving home discussing the situation . . . again. Out of the backseat came the voice of our ten-year-old daughter: "God will provide." Arriving at home, she went to the mailbox to pick up the mail. She handed an envelope to me. I opened the envelope to find a check. I was speechless. My husband was watching me and asked, "What's wrong now?" We had had a rough several months. When I could muster my voice, I told him, "You need to sit down!" With a strange look on his face, he sat down and reached for the letter. It contained a check for $5,000. By then, we were all speechless as we cried and praised God!

- I came to your meeting. I had no money and had just lost my business. I had just started a new job and had just gotten my first paycheck. At offering time, God told me to give $100. I argued with Him. "That's all I have left for the electricity bill!" He repeated Himself: "Give it!" Thankfully, I was obedient to His voice and gave all I had in that offering. When the next electricity bill arrived in May, I really thought they made a mistake. It said I owed nothing. Nothing! Needless to say, I praised God! The June, July, and August bills arrived and reported the same amount due: NOTHING! Houston summers are HOT! The bills should have totaled well over $1,000. God paid the bill! Hallelujah!

- About three years ago (2016), I was in one of your meetings where you taught on scriptural giving. I seeded $111 in the offering for my daughter as you instructed. My daughter had her heart set on attending Liberty University. Due to the expense of the university, she was going to go to the local college for two years and then transfer to Liberty. I was going to sell our home and move back to Grandma's house. My son had been saving money for several years to buy a truck. He volunteered to give her his savings so she could at least start her college education. About two weeks after your meeting, an acquaintance came into the store to shop. She asked me if my daughter wanted to go to college. Of course, I said, "Yes, she really wants to go to Liberty University." The lady took out her checkbook and wrote a check for $60,000 to cover the entire four years! My daughter graduated last May with honors from Liberty University! Debt-free! In addition, I didn't have to sell the house and move in with Grandma. My son didn't have to give up his savings. But the story doesn't end there. My son did buy his truck and ended up trading it for a used Jeep a few years later. As he was driving one day, he could hear someone screaming, "HELP!" He stopped to help and found someone stuck in a ditch which was filling up with water. It was apparent the person would drown if something wasn't done quickly. My son remembered that a life preserver had been left in the back of the Jeep. He grabbed the preserver, threw it to the person, and pulled them to safety. Think about all the details that had to be in place for God's plan to come together. My daughter got her education, and my son got his vehicle and was in the right place at the right time to save someone's life! God is so good!

This is the season for debt cancellations. God is cancelling, discounting, or paying off car loans, home mortgages, and other debts. Believe God for his miracle of provision. Expect it! Plan for it! And let us know when it happens.

Pray this prayer:

Thank you, Father, for the bountiful blessings you have poured over my life. You have never left me without food or drink. I have lived this long because you have supplied my needs. Praise you, Lord. You are such a good Father. In Jesus's name. Amen.

7

Miracle of Healing

Miracles of healing are some of the most inspiring stories in the Bible. You may be able to think of several stories off the top of your head where people came to Jesus begging to be healed. One of the reasons these stories are so moving is because where there is a need for healing, there is usually great sorrow and great loss. And to see people reunited with their families and communities to live their lives fully again is a beautiful thing. Most of us have experienced a time when a family member or friend has suffered from a disease or illness, and we long to see them healed and made whole. This situation was nearly commonplace during Jesus's three years of earthly ministry. In fact, people heard about his miracles of healing and would travel great distances to be in his presence. They would follow him from town to town just to witness these great miracles. Surely it was awe-inspiring. But the miracle of healing didn't begin with Jesus's ministry. God was actually healing people long before Jesus was born.

Miracle Healing in the Old Testament

From as early as Genesis and throughout the Old Testament, God revealed himself time and again as a God who heals. In Exodus, God issued a decree for the Israelites, saying, "If you will listen carefully to the voice of the Lord your God and do what is right in his sight, obeying his commands and keeping all his decrees, then I will not make you suffer any of the diseases I sent on the Egyptians; for I am the Lord who heals you" (Exodus 15:26 NLT).

Later in the Old Testament, the psalmist writes, "Some people became fools and turned against God, and they suffered for the evil they did. They became so sick that they refused to eat, so they almost died. They were in trouble, so they called to the Lord for help, and he saved them from their troubles. He gave the command and healed them, so they were saved from the grave" (Psalm 107:17–20 ERV).

Clearly, God desired to heal his people. But let's look at some specific stories where God's miracle of healing truly changed people's lives in the Old Testament.

The Healing of Naaman

If we look at the story of Naaman in the Old Testament, we find a very interesting account. Naaman was the commander of the king's army. He was someone in authority who wanted and, I am sure, demanded respect. When he learned that Elisha was healing people, he sent a message to Elisha indicating he desired a meeting. Naaman had leprosy, and he wanted to see this man of God so that he could be healed. He traveled all the way to Elisha's house and stood outside the door. Only instead of coming outside to meet with Naaman, Elisha simply sent his messenger outside with instructions. This very impersonal reply was an insult to the commander. But his servants convinced him to obey, and when he did, he received the healing he needed: "And Elisha sent a messenger to him, saying, 'Go and wash in the Jordan seven times, and your flesh shall be restored to you, and you shall be clean.' . . . So he went down and dipped seven times in the Jordan, according to the saying of the man of God; and his flesh was restored like the flesh of a little child, and he was clean" (2 Kings 5:10, 14 NKJV).

Upon coming out of the water the seventh time and seeing his skin as clear as a young child's, Naaman must have felt surprised and humbled. He regretted his initial anger toward Elisha, responding with gratitude toward him and acknowledging that Naaman's God was the only God in the entire world. What a change of heart!

The Healing of Hezekiah

Another story of Old Testament healing happened to King Hezekiah. At one time, Hezekiah became gravely ill, almost to the point of death. God sent the prophet Isaiah to tell Hezekiah to put his house in order because he was not going to recover from this illness, and he would soon die. When Hezekiah heard this, he prayed to God and wept. And the God of all miracles heard Hezekiah's prayer.

It happened, before Isaiah had gone out into the middle court, that the word of the LORD came to him, saying, "Return and tell Hezekiah the leader of My people, 'Thus says the LORD, the God of David your father: I have heard your prayer, I have seen your tears; surely I will heal you. On the third day you shall go up to the house of the LORD. And I will add to your days fifteen years.'"
(2 Kings 20:4–6 NKJV)

Then Isaiah told Hezekiah to take a lump of figs and place it on a boil on his skin, and Hezekiah was healed. What must it feel like to hear God tell you that you are going to die, then to pray to God and have him hear your prayers and give you fifteen more years of life? Hezekiah must have been overwhelmed with gratitude for this great gift! What a blessing to serve a God who can not only heal us but who listens to our heart's yearnings and our prayers!

Miracle Healing in the New Testament

This type of miraculous healing continued into and throughout the New Testament with Jesus and his disciples. And even after Jesus's ascension into heaven, the disciples and followers of Jesus continued ministering to and healing the sick.

- Jesus went about all Galilee, teaching in their synagogues, preaching the gospel of the kingdom, and healing all kinds of sickness and all kinds of disease among the people. (Matthew 4:23 NKJV)

- Jesus reached out his hand and touched the leper and said, "Of course I want to heal you—be healed!" And instantly, all signs of leprosy disappeared! (Matthew 8:3 TPT)

- When Jesus knew it, He withdrew from there. And great multitudes followed Him, and He healed them all. (Matthew 12:15 NKJV)

- Great multitudes came to Him, having with them the lame, blind, mute, maimed, and many others; and they laid them down at Jesus's feet, and He healed them. So the multitude marveled when they saw the mute speaking, the maimed made whole, the lame walking, and the blind seeing; and they glorified the God of Israel. (Matthew 15:30–31 NKJV)

- He came to Bethsaida; and they brought a blind man to Him, and begged Him to touch him. So He took the blind man by the hand and led him out of the town. And when He had spit on his eyes and put His hands on him, He asked him if he saw anything. And he looked up and said, "I see men like trees, walking." Then He put His hands on his eyes again and made him look up. And he was restored and saw everyone clearly. (Mark 8:22–25 NKJV)

- When [Jesus] had looked around at them all, He said to the man, "Stretch out your hand." And he did so, and his hand was restored as whole as the other. (Luke 6:10 NKJV)

The Healing of the Bleeding Woman

One of the most powerful stories in Scripture is that of the bleeding woman who came to Jesus for healing. You should study the entire story to get the whole picture. But consider this: A lady had been very sick for many years and had lost hope of ever being healed. In that culture at that time, her issue of bleeding required her to stay home and away from other people. The law of that day allowed anyone to stone her if they discovered her out in public. She risked her life to get to Jesus and to receive her miracle. Read what Mark and Luke wrote in their gospels:

- She said, "If only I may touch His clothes I shall be made well." (Mark 5:28 NKJV)

- When the woman saw that she was not hidden, she came trembling; and falling down before Him, she declared to Him in the presence of all the people the reason she had touched Him and how she was healed immediately. (Luke 8:47 NKJV)

- He said to her, "Daughter, your faith has made you well. Go in peace. Your suffering is over." (Mark 5:34 NLT)

This very determined lady got what she was seeking. She risked everything—her very life—to get to her Savior. If you are in need of healing, would you be willing to do the same? What are you willing to do to receive your miracle and be healed?

The Healing of the Lepers

On one occasion, a group of lepers sought Jesus for the miracle of healing. This took great courage and a huge leap of faith, but they got what they were seeking. The one leper who came back to say thank you to Jesus was not just healed of the leprosy; he was then made whole (Luke 17:19 KJV), meaning his missing body parts were restored. His missing fingers and toes were placed back on his hands and feet, like new.

So this group whose disease had eaten away their fingers, toes, and most likely other body appendages, and who faced ultimate death were given life. And even better, this group who had been isolated, rejected, and feared by others was now healed and able to rejoin their families, talk to their friends, and hug their loved ones. Imagine the joy! Talk about a miracle!

More New Testament Healings

Story after story in the New Testament reveals the miracle of healing by Jesus and his disciples. People came to Jesus and the disciples, putting action to their faith. They longed to be healed, and when they were, they praised God for all he had done in their lives!

- When Jesus stopped to look at them, he spoke these words: "Go to be examined by the Jewish priests." They set off, and they were healed while walking along the way. (Luke 17:14 TPT)

- Only then did Jesus answer the question posed by John's disciples. "Now go back and tell John what you have just seen and heard here today. The blind are now seeing. The crippled are now walking. Those who were lepers are now cured. Those who were deaf are now hearing. Those who were dead are now raised back to life. The poor and broken are given the hope of salvation." (Luke 7:22 TPT)

- When Jesus saw him lying there, he knew that the man had been crippled for a long time. So Jesus said to him, "Do you truly long to be healed?" The sick man answered him, "Sir, there's no way I can get healed, for I have no one who will lower me into the water when the angel comes. As soon as I try to crawl to the edge of the pool, someone else jumps in ahead of me." Then Jesus said to him, "Stand up! Pick up your sleeping mat and you will walk!" Immediately he stood up—he was healed! So he rolled up his mat and walked again! (John 5:6–9 TPT)

- A huge crowd kept following him wherever he went, because they saw his miraculous signs as he healed the sick. (John 6:2 NLT)

- Jesus spat on the ground and made some clay with his saliva. Then he anointed the blind man's eyes with the clay. And he said to the blind man, "Now go and wash the clay from your eyes in the ritual pool of Siloam." So he went and washed his face and as he came back, he could see for the first time in his life! (John 9:6–7 TPT)

- Peter said, "Silver and gold I do not have, but what I do have I give you: In the name of Jesus Christ of Nazareth, rise up and walk." And he took him by the right hand and lifted him up, and immediately his feet and ankle bones received strength. So he, leaping up, stood and walked and entered the temple with them—walking, leaping, and praising God. (Acts 3:6–8 NKJV)

- Everyone was praising God for this wonderful miracle—the healing of a man who had been lame for forty years.
  (Acts 4:21–22 TLB)

- Philip went down to the city of Samaria, and preached Christ unto them. And the people with one accord gave heed unto those things which Philip spake, hearing and seeing the miracles which he did. For unclean spirits, crying with loud voice, came out of many that were possessed with them: and many taken with palsies, and that were lame, were healed.
  (Acts 8:5–7 KJV)

- God spoke the words "Be healed," and we were healed, delivered from death's door!
  (Psalm 107:20 TPT)

The Power of Prayer Cloths

During Christian conventions or conferences, you may have heard the term *prayer cloths*. These are special pieces of fabric that are cut into two to three-inch squares and prayed over. Then the anointed cloths are passed out to anyone who wants one. They are easy to carry in a Bible, pocket, or billfold. They are also easy to stick under someone's pillow who needs a touch from God. Even the Bible mentions the use of cloths in healing: "Now God worked unusual miracles by the hands of Paul, so that even handkerchiefs or aprons were brought from his body to the sick, and the diseases left them and the evil spirits went out of them" (Acts 19:11–12 NKJV).

Just like in this verse, any type of fabric can be anointed for this purpose. In this biblical account, people used handkerchiefs or aprons, but a prayer cloth can be made of any type of fabric. For instance, we have specially made "Miracles Happen!" blankets that my staff and I pray over. There are even pink and blue ones for babies. Special green throws are designed specifically for veterans. People can sleep under one of our throws while soaking in God's anointing as they rest. We have received many testimonies of healings from people who have used prayer cloths or blankets.

One veteran has had PTSD for dozens of years. Nightmares were a common occurrence. He was miserable until I prayed for him and sent him home with a green "Miracles Happen!" throw. His nightmares have ceased! Now he loves to smile, share his testimony, and pray for others. He now ministers to veterans, first responders, and others who suffer with PTSD.

Another great story came in from a military wife. She knew God could heal her spouse from the PTSD that had tortured him and the effects on the whole family. She took home a green "Miracles Happen!" throw. She didn't tell him about the meeting or what to expect from the blanket. Before he went to sleep, she carefully placed the blanket under the sheets. Every morning, he woke up better than the day before. Jesus has healed him. Praise God!

A lady came forward for prayer. She did not have working saliva glands and had to get up at night to drink in order to prevent further complications in her mouth. After sleeping under an anointed throw for several nights, her saliva glands are back to normal and, as a bonus, she also received healing for her sleep apnea. Hallelujah!

Testimonies of the Miracle of Healing

Amazing testimonies of healing miracles come into the ministry office daily via phone, mail, or email. The one common thread throughout any healing testimony is the willingness of the recipient. No one can force healing upon another. In the case of children, the parents have to be the willing participant. Adults must take a step of faith for themselves. One young lady was very sick. She claimed she was too sick to come to a meeting for healing prayers and ministry. This was a prime example of a person in need who was unwilling to put action to her faith. I often wonder what would have happened had she moved mountains to come to that healing meeting.

Then there were plenty of others who did take that step of faith:

One woman suffered with lupus and severe fibromyalgia. She heard about Joan Hunter Ministries and searched for my videos on YouTube. She watched every video she could find until she felt well enough to come to a meeting. Even then, she and her husband had to drive four hours to get to the church sponsoring the healing service. She put action to her faith, got prayed for, and was gloriously healed. Now she and her spouse travel with me and assist during services.

One man who had been bitten by a fox came for prayer. I prayed against the trauma and contamination as well as for total healing. He was completely healed and left praising God. His wife wrote to our ministry: "When Joan was here in 2017, she prayed for my retired military husband who had been bitten by a rabid fox on a military base. He had to get a lengthy series of rabies shots with human DNA. Joan broke off any 'curses' that were in the DNA injections."

And once, a lady came into our office who had received a diagnosis of terminal cancer. I prayed. She saw her doctor a few weeks later. I received an excited call shortly after that visit. She was deemed 100 percent cancer-free. Only God can perform a miracle like that!

Of all the testimonies of miracle healing that come through our office, one man's story really stands out. He was suffering from debilitating pain from performing over four hundred parachute jumps and damaging his lower back and knees. His wife shared his story of healing:

The Holy Spirit immediately began "tingling" in my husband's lower back for about forty-five seconds. He described the feeling like hundreds of little knitting needles inside mending his lower back. Then, the knitting-needle, tingling feeling hit both of his knees for about fifteen seconds.

God dramatically healed him that day. He began increasing his exercise. However, he discovered that his hip joints had also been damaged from the parachute jumps, and with his lower back and knees healed, his hip joints began to ache with the exercise.

So, when Joan came back later that year, a member from her team prayed directly for my husband's hips. Although it seemed that nothing dramatic happened during that prayer (he did not feel anything), the next morning his hips were fine! Praise the Lord! All the joint pain from years of parachute jumps was gone!

He has been able to return to exercising and running approximately six to eight miles three to five times a week for the last year! Praise the Lord! I pray that this testimony encourages Joan and her team to keep praying for those in pain! To God be the glory! Sometimes God releases healing in a dramatic way and other times not dramatic, but when the fruit of healing comes, we praise his holy name!
—Blessings! KM and VM, monthly partners

Christians have documented healings throughout the centuries. I have seen and ministered healing to countless thousands since I started praying for the sick some forty-five years ago. Even doctors have documented healings they didn't understand. Expect them to happen to you, and praise God for every miracle he blesses you with. Whatever you are believing God for, take a step of faith and prepare yourself to receive. Cry out to God! He does answer. Pray for your miraculous healing right now.

Pray this prayer:

Father, I believe you can heal me of _____ right here and right now. I speak miraculous healing to every cell in my body. I reach out to you, Jesus, to work through me to not only heal me but also to heal others through me. Thank you, Jesus, for your miracles in my life. In Jesus's name. Amen.

Healing Long Distance

We all know Jesus laid hands on the sick and people recovered, but he had many ways of healing the sick. He often prayed in person, but several stories indicate his word went before him and healed many others also. One of those stories appears in John's Gospel and it tells of a government official who asks Jesus to heal his dying son:

> Jesus entered the village of Cana of Galilee where he had transformed water into wine. And there was a governmental official in Capernaum who had a son who was very sick and dying. When he heard that Jesus had left Judea and was staying in Cana of

Galilee, he decided to make the journey to Cana. When he found Jesus, he begged him, "You must come with me to Capernaum and heal my son!"

So Jesus said to him, "You never believe unless you see signs and wonders."

But the man continued to plead, "You have to come with me to Capernaum before my little boy dies!"

Then Jesus looked him in the eyes and said, "Go back home now. I promise you, your son will live and not die."

The man believed in his heart the words of Jesus and set off for home. When he was still a distance from Capernaum, his servants met him on the road and told him the good news, "Your son is healed! He's alive!"

Overjoyed, the father asked his servants, "When did my son begin to recover?"

"Yesterday," they said, "at one in the afternoon. All at once his fever broke—and now he's well!"

Then the father realized that it was at that very same hour that Jesus spoke the words to him, "Your son will live and not die." So from that day forward, the man and all his family and servants believed. This was Jesus' second extraordinary miracle in Galilee after coming from Judea.
(John 4:46–54 TPT)

Just like Jesus sent his word of healing to reach the sick, you and I can do the same. If you are a believer, Jesus lives within you. Your words are his as you pray for others, whether nearby or miles across the globe. They are equally powerful in person or long distance. Pray in agreement and send his angels to the one you are praying for. Believe your words have the same power as Jesus's words did.

What are you willing to do to see your miracle happen? Be obedient to God's instructions and put action to your faith.

Many calls for prayer come from around the world. On a daily basis, phone lines as well as the internet carry healing prayers by our prayer partners. And just as many people report testimonies using the same communication tools. Words are powerful no matter what means of communication you use. Letters work also, but they are just much slower. I request the person who gets a letter or email to speak the prayers aloud so the person needing healing can hear the prayers as well as read them. I also ask that you speak the prayers in this book aloud so you can hear them.

The Joan Hunter Ministry office receives hundreds of calls every week. Some are requesting prayer for their needs; however, many other calls are to report a testimony of their miracles from watching my TV show or attending a meeting in the past. Many testimonies of miraculous healings can also be found in my books: *How to Heal the Whole Man*, *Power to Heal*, and *Healing Starts Now*. We cannot discount or ignore the hundreds of miracle testimonies we get every week. You can call us anytime and get your healing long distance also. Will your testimony be the next one we receive? I hope so!

Pray this prayer:

Father, let my words be your words. Let my prayers come straight from your heart to travel across the miles to reach whomever I am praying for. May I always be obedient to your promptings to pray for others in need. In Jesus's name. Amen.

Deliverance from Demon Spirits

Jesus recognized spirits who came from the enemy. The devil's intentions were to rob, kill, and destroy, but Jesus's goal was the exact opposite. He wanted people walking in freedom and love. Casting out demons was one thing Jesus did often during his ministry, and the Bible documents numerous accounts. The most dramatic is when Jesus delivered the man in the cemetery from many demons:

> There met Him out of the tombs a
> man with an unclean spirit, who had
> his dwelling among the tombs; and
> no one could bind him, not even with
> chains, because he had often been
> bound with shackles and chains. And

the chains had been pulled apart by
him, and the shackles broken in pieces; neither could anyone tame him.
And always, night and day, he was
in the mountains and in the tombs,
crying out and cutting himself with
stones. (Mark 5:2–5 NKJV)

When the man saw Jesus, he ran to him and worshiped him. Then Jesus commanded the unclean spirit to
come out of the man, and he cast the demons into a herd of
swine: "Now a large herd of swine was feeding there near
the mountains. So all the demons begged Him, saying,
'Send us to the swine, that we may enter them.' And at once
Jesus gave them permission. Then the unclean spirits went
out and entered the swine (there were about two thousand); and the herd ran violently down the steep place into
the sea, and drowned in the sea" (Mark 5: 11–13 NKJV).

There were many other Gospel accounts of Jesus
casting out demons:

- He healed many who were sick with various diseases, and cast out many demons;
  and He did not allow the demons to speak,
  because they knew Him. (Mark 1:34 NKJV)

- When He rose early on the first day of the week, He appeared first to Mary Magdalene, out of whom He had cast seven demons. (Mark 16:9 NKJV)

- Eyewitnesses to the miracle reported all that they had seen and how the demonized man was completely delivered from his torment. After hearing about such amazing power, the townspeople became frightened. (Luke 8:36 TPT)

- Many demon-possessed people were set free and delivered as evil spirits came out of them with loud screams and shrieks, and many who were lame and paralyzed were also healed. (Acts 8:7 TPT)

Jesus was given power and authority to destroy the enemy. And since Jesus lives within us, we have that same authority. Even Jesus's disciples learned how to minister deliverance by using his name. You and I can also use Jesus's name when we encounter the enemy. Jesus gave us permission to put his name in our arsenal of weapons to fight the battle. When you are faced with an attack, remember to use the name of Jesus. You will gain the ultimate victory!

- Jesus came close to them and said, "All the authority of the universe has been given to me." (Matthew 28:18 TPT)

- Jesus called his twelve disciples to him and gave them authority to cast out evil spirits and to heal every kind of sickness and disease. (Matthew 10:1 TLB) (Also see Luke 9:1.)

- The seventy returned with joy, saying, "Lord, even the demons are subject to us in Your name." (Luke 10:17 NKJV)

No one should approach deliverance lightly. It is not the same as praying for a disease or provision. You should be trained and always have a partner and back-up prayers protecting you. Even the disciples had to be trained before being successful with this area of ministry. Get prepared before fighting this battle. Some diseases that prayers do not heal may have some evil spirits attached to the person. Learn how to handle these situations.

Testimony of Healing and Deliverance

Recently, a lady came to one of our services. She had experienced tremendous trauma through the years. She had an abusive childhood and an abusive ex-spouse, which resulted in post-traumatic stress disorder and a traumatic brain injury. She couldn't think clearly from the brain damage. I prayed for her, of course. Instantly, she felt something leave her. Her eyes were bright and shining, and there was life in her voice. She was so totally changed. Her husband barely recognized her when he came to pick her up.

God can heal our most painful trauma and can give us life in its place! Never discount your testimony of what God has done for you. Yes, it may scare some people. They may say you are crazy; however, you know what God has done for you. Stick to your story. A testimony can open spiritually blind eyes to his Word. A testimony can be a very strong motivation for the unsaved to come to Jesus and be healed.

Throughout the New Testament stories, people who had witnessed the miracles of Jesus and his followers and who had been disobedient were scared. Seeing God's power through Jesus, they repented for their sins and cried out to God. The things they saw changed them! How could they not? Amazing miracles happened then. And amazing healing miracles still happen today.

Pray this prayer:

Father, I need your wisdom and discernment when encountering challenging situations. Give me the words to speak, Father, your words to successfully win the earthly battles I face. Let me understand what to do and when to do it. In Jesus's name. Amen.

8

Miracle of Resurrection

When someone mentions or uses the term *resurrection*, my first thought is of Jesus, my Lord and Savior who gave his life for me. But he did not stop in the grave. Three days later, he woke up, folded the grave clothes neatly, and walked out of his grave very much alive. In and through Jesus, you and I have that same miracle waiting for us. When we die in this world, we will be very much alive in heaven.

The prophecies spoken over a thousand years before Jesus was born told of the miracles that would occur during his birth, life, and death. The manifestations of ancient prophecies were miracles in and of themselves. God gave his prophets hints about his Son, the Messiah, to give his children hope. And he is still doing that today. His Word tells us what is to come and offers hope through Jesus's miraculous resurrection. We can know without a doubt that God's Word is truth. Death on earth is not final. Jesus came back to tell us and show us that he opened the door to his Father's kingdom for us. Everything about Jesus's life and death is a miracle, and we get to share in that with him.

Truly, the resurrection of Jesus is one of the greatest miracles of all time! It's definitely the most talked about and celebrated resurrections shared in God's Word. But there are other stories in both the Old and New Testaments where ordinary people were resurrected from the dead.

Elijah Raises a Young Boy from the Dead

Let's look first at the story of Elijah who brought a young boy from death back to life:

One day the woman's son became sick and died. "O man of God," she cried, "what have you done to me? Have you come here to punish my sins by killing my son?" "Give him to me," Elijah replied. And he took the boy's body from her and carried it upstairs to the guest room where he lived, and laid the body on his bed, and then cried out to the Lord, "O Lord my God, why have you killed the son of this widow with whom I am staying?" And he stretched himself upon the child three times and cried out to the Lord, "O Lord my God, please let this child's spirit return to him." And the Lord heard Elijah's prayer; and the spirit of the child returned, and he became alive again! Then Elijah took him downstairs and gave him to his mother. "See! He's alive!" he beamed. (1 Kings 17:17–23 TLB)

This is the same widow to whom God sent Elijah, and whom Elijah had saved from starvation by performing a miracle with the flour and oil. What confusion this mother must have felt when the son who was saved from starvation then died! She knew enough to ask for help in the right place. Instead of going into mourning, she showed her respect and belief in Elijah's position as God's prophet and knew that he was capable of miracles.

Elijah didn't panic at the news of the boy's death. He took the child and immediately called out to God, asking him to return the boy's spirit to his lifeless body. God transferred life into the boy, and his spirit returned. Can you imagine the mother's surprise upon witnessing a second miracle performed by Elijah—the first with flour and oil and the second in resurrecting her beloved son? Surely her faith in God must have soared.

Jesus Raises Lazarus from the Dead

One of the most memorable resurrection stories is that of Jesus raising Lazarus from the dead. Mary and Martha were distraught over the death of their brother, who was also Jesus's dear friend. But Jesus. He did not begin grieving at this news. No. Instead, Jesus called

Lazarus from the tomb where he had been dead for four days:

> Jesus said, "Take away the stone." Martha, the sister of him who was dead, said to Him, "Lord, by this time there is a stench, for he has been dead four days." Jesus said to her, "Did I not say to you that if you would believe you would see the glory of God?" Then they took away the stone from the place where the dead man was lying. And Jesus lifted up His eyes and said, "Father, I thank You that You have heard Me. And I know that You always hear Me, but because of the people who are standing by I said this, that they may believe that You sent Me." Now when He had said these things, He cried with a loud voice, "Lazarus, come forth!" And he who had died came out bound hand and foot with graveclothes, and his face was wrapped with a cloth. Jesus said

to them, "Loose him, and let him go."
(John 11:39–44 NKJV)

In this situation, see the power in the words of Jesus. He spoke to the situation with all the authority of God. He prayed with very specific words. If Jesus hadn't been specific using the name of Lazarus, other dead bodies may have also come forth.

Peter Raises Tabitha

Then in Acts, we find the story of Tabitha, or Dorcas, whom Peter restores to life. Using the same authority that Jesus spoke to raise Lazarus, Peter spoke to raise Tabitha:

At Joppa there was a certain disciple named Tabitha, which is translated Dorcas. This woman was full of good works and charitable deeds which she did. But it happened in those days that she became sick and died. When they had washed her, they laid her in an upper room. And since Lydda was near Joppa, and the disciples had heard that Peter was there, they sent two men to him, imploring him not to delay in coming to them. Then Peter arose and went with them. When he had come, they brought him to the upper room. And all the widows stood by him weeping, showing the tunics and garments which Dorcas had made while she was with them. But Peter put them all out, and knelt down and prayed. And turning to the body he said, "Tabitha, arise." And she opened her eyes, and when she saw Peter she sat up. Then he gave her his hand and lifted her up; and when he had called the saints and widows, he presented her alive. And it became known throughout all Joppa, and many believed on the Lord. (Acts 9:36–42 NKJV)

It's not difficult to imagine the surprise and joy of the other widows to see their dear friend come to life again. You might also imagine the excitement as the news of this miracle spread throughout their town. Peter, through the power and authority of God, had brought this beloved woman back to life.

Jesus Raises a Young Girl

And, finally, there is the story of the synagogue ruler's daughter. The ruler knew if there was any hope for his daughter, it was with Jesus.

> While He was still speaking, some came from the ruler of the synagogue's house who said, "Your daughter is dead. Why trouble the Teacher any further?" As soon as Jesus heard the word that was spoken, He said to the ruler of the synagogue, "Do not be afraid; only believe." And He permitted no one to follow Him except Peter, James, and John the brother of James. Then He came to the house of the ruler of the synagogue, and saw a tumult and those who wept and wailed loudly. When He came in, He said to them, "Why make this commotion and weep? The child is not dead,

but sleeping." And they ridiculed Him. But when He had put them all outside, He took the father and the mother of the child, and those who were with Him, and entered where the child was lying. Then He took the child by the hand, and said to her, "Talitha, cumi," which is translated, "Little girl, I say to you, arise." Immediately the girl arose and walked, for she was twelve years of age. And they were overcome with great amazement. (Mark 5:35–42 NKJV)

What a miracle for these grieving parents! To have their daughter who they thought to be dead—who *was* dead—to be brought back to life.

In these last two resurrection stories, there is something important to note. Look at them again and notice that both Jesus and Peter removed the unbelievers from the scene. If Jesus chose not to minister healing with the doubters nearby, remember that you and I probably won't have success with such scoffers. Likewise, Jesus couldn't perform miracles aside from a few healings in his hometown because the people didn't believe. Learning from these examples of Jesus and Peter, you must remember to surround yourself with people in agreement with you in every area, not just healing. You may have to handle serious situations privately to optimize God's healing power

The Miracle of Resurrection Today

Consider the fact that even a baby is born spiritually dead. During that child's lifetime, someone has to open his or her eyes and heart to God's light and entrance into eternal life through Jesus Christ. New Christians are often referred to as *baby Christians*. Babies have much to learn no matter what age they may be. The spiritually dead walk by us daily. If you are a believer in Jesus, you carry the answer, the key, to the door to heaven. You have to commit to raising the dead around you by sharing Jesus with them.

Finally, resurrection from physical death is not the only thing that needs to come to life. What dreams and visions do you have? What about business ideas? Are there goals you have left on the shelf? Resurrect these ideas and bring them back to life. Resurrect your dreams and visions. Let God show you what to do to breathe energy into every area of your life. He can cause everything to soar!

Look beyond your circumstances to the truth. What is God trying to do in your situation? How and what is God trying to raise to life in you? Being tuned in to his Holy Spirit is so important. Follow his instructions and speak his words. The dead can come back to life.

Pray this prayer:

Father, allow my eyes and ears to be sensitive to people around me. Show me the spiritually dead and allow me to minister your light and life to them through your love, your joy, and your Word. Let me share the miracle of life with them. Thank you, Father, for breathing life into my dreams and visions. Thank you for resurrecting ideas I thought were impossible. Let me walk in your will. In Jesus's name. Amen.

9

Miracle of Conception

Throughout history, God has used the miracle of conception to surprise his children and to carry out his plan for his creation. If you've ever known someone who has struggled and grieved over infertility or miscarriage, you know it's heartbreaking and life-altering. The one thing some couples want most in the world—a child—isn't happening or is taken from them. But God. He cares and he loves us. He knows our sorrows and our longings, and he wants to give us the desires of our heart. He wants to give life to those he loves. Let's look at some of the miracle stories of conception in God's Word.

Old Testament Miracles of Conception

The Bible documents several miraculous conceptions. Let's look first at some in the Old Testament. After many petitions to God, faithful women were blessed with children. One of those women was Sarah, the wife of Abraham. When Abraham was ninety-nine years old, God promised him that he would be the father of many nations and that Sarah would birth a child. What joy and surprise they must have felt!

- Abraham fell on his face and laughed, and said in his heart, "Shall a child be born to a man who is one hundred years old? And shall Sarah, who is ninety years old, bear a child?" (Genesis 17:17 NKJV)

- Sarah conceived and bore Abraham a son in his old age, at the set time of which God had spoken to him. (Genesis 21:2 NKJV)

God truly has a sense of humor giving a one-hundred-year-old man and a ninety-year-old woman a baby! But oh, the joy! How grateful they must have been when they held God's promise in their arms! Sarah, who had been barren for ninety years, was now a mother!

Hannah was another woman who desperately wanted a baby and cried out to God for a miracle. She would go to the temple and pray, moving her mouth but not uttering any words. Her odd behavior made Eli, the priest, think she was drunk. But she shared her sorrow with Eli, and he said to her, "Go in peace, and the God of Israel grant your petition which you have asked of Him" (1 Samuel 1:17 NKJV). Hannah went home, ate, and believed his word. She put action to her faith, she trusted God, and God answered her prayers. She conceived, and Samuel was born: "So it came to pass in the process of time that Hannah conceived and bore a son, and called his name Samuel, saying, 'Because I have asked for him from the Lord'" (1 Samuel 1:20 NKJV). Many women can relate to Hannah's prayers in the temple. May we find comfort in knowing that God hears every word. And may we have courage to share our sorrows and desires with those who can pray with us and petition God on our behalf.

Rachel, the wife of Jacob, is yet another woman who wanted a child. She prayed to God, he listened to her prayers, and she conceived a son: "Then God remembered Rachel; he listened to her and enabled her to conceive. She became pregnant and gave birth to a son and said, 'God has taken away my disgrace.' She named him Joseph, and said, 'May the LORD add to me another son.'" (Genesis 30:22–24 NIV). During this time, there was great shame in not being able to conceive and birth a child. Rachel must have felt less than other women. Her longing wasn't just to have a child. It was to redeem her social standing as well. And God heard her prayer. He listened and gave her the longing of her heart.

In 2 Kings, we find a story of a prominent woman whose husband was old. The couple had been kind to the prophet Elisha, giving him a place to stay whenever he was in their town. The woman desperately wanted to conceive a child. When she shared her grief with Elisha, he prophesied over her, telling her that God would answer her prayer: "When she returned, he talked to her as she stood in the doorway. 'Next year at about this time you shall have a son!' 'O man of God,' she exclaimed, 'don't lie to me like that!' But it was true; the woman soon conceived and had a baby boy the following year, just as Elisha had predicted" (2 Kings 4:16–17 TLB). This woman and her elderly husband must have been overjoyed at this news. Not only did God heal this woman's body so that she could conceive, but he healed her broken heart and replaced her grief with great joy! Miracle upon miracle!

New Testament Miracles of Conception

Before Mary's most miraculous conception in the New Testament, Elizabeth, Mary's cousin, was unable to have children. Elizabeth and her husband, Zacharias, had long prayed for a child. But God. He had a plan. He would give Elizabeth the desire of her heart and use her child in a mighty way.

> But they had no children, for Elizabeth was barren; and now they were both very old. . . . But the angel said, "Don't be afraid, Zacharias! For I have come to tell you that God has heard your prayer, and your wife, Elizabeth, will bear you a son! . . . And you are to name him John." Soon afterwards Elizabeth his wife became pregnant and

went into seclusion for five months.…
"Furthermore, six months ago your
Aunt Elizabeth—'the barren one,' they
called her—became pregnant in her
old age!" (Luke 1:7, 13, 24, 36)

God had a plan and a purpose for Elizabeth and her son. This baby would grow up to become John the Baptist, Jesus's cousin, who helped usher in the ministry of the long-awaited Savior. Truly God's plans are greater than we could ever imagine!

The Virgin Birth

One of the best-known miracles of conception in the Bible surrounds the birth of Jesus. Matthew writes in his Gospel, "These are the facts concerning the birth of Jesus Christ: His mother, Mary, was engaged to be married to Joseph. But while she was still a virgin she became pregnant by the Holy Spirit" (Matthew 1:18 TLB). A virgin birth had never occurred before and has never repeated itself since. A visit from an angel must have caused quite a stir among Mary's neighbors, friends, and family. Rumors must have flown about this unexpected pregnancy. They probably questioned her sanity; they certainly must have questioned her integrity.

Amazingly, Joseph's visit by another angel convinced him of Mary's chastity and purity. Matthew writes, "As he lay awake considering this, he fell into a dream, and saw an angel standing beside him. 'Joseph, son of David,' the angel said, 'don't hesitate to take Mary as your wife! For the child within her has been conceived by the Holy Spirit'" (Matthew 1:20 TLB).

More than one miracle happened even before the blessed night of Jesus's birth in Bethlehem. Getting Mary to Bethlehem to fulfill the age-old prophecy, arranging the wise men's arrival after traveling for months, and inviting the shepherds to that blessed manger all had to have supernatural planning which only God could have done (see Micah 5:2).

God answered prayers and blessed these faithful people with offspring. And he can do the same today. If you want a child, prepare yourself by reading these stories over and over, pray, and believe for your miracle! Allow your faith to grow. Don't give up. Exercise your faith. Put action to your prayers. We have to participate and work out what needs to be done before birthing any dream, but many people don't want to do what it takes to receive their miracle. Revelation must be birthed inside of you. This is conception time.

Testimonies of Miracle Conception

We receive many stories of people who have struggled for years to have children, and how God answers their prayers. Here are a few of those stories:

> At an ordination class which we hold twice a year during our healing school, my husband, Kelley, gave a word about babies. He also said to ask you to pray for me. I found you outside in the lobby . . . and you prayed for me and gave me a pair of baby booties. You told me to send you a picture of the baby in the booties after the baby arrived. At the age of forty-five, after twenty-one years of marriage and infertility, and three international adoptions, baby Andy arrived on November 2, 2018. He is doing well, and we are praising God. Enclosed please find his picture.

Thank you from the bottom of my heart. Miracles Happen! —Love, W

*****

You prayed over us when you came to the UK. God blessed us with a baby boy on May 22. Our testimony follows. I had faith that God would make the impossible things possible. My name is Pretty, but my life was not that beautiful. We did not have any children after seven years of married life. I was depressed. I had had three miscarriages, including one ectopic pregnancy. I lost a tube, and after that, my chance of getting pregnant was reduced by 50 percent. We were longing to hold our own baby in our hands, and we were praying for a miracle. Our church members were also praying earnestly for us.

I have received many prophecies through different men of God that God will answer my prayers as Hannah in the Bible. In December 2017, my husband and myself had an opportunity to attend a prayer meeting where the message preached was about Jesus Christ who could do supernatural things for us. After the prayer meeting, I had faith that God would make the impossible things possible. You prayed for me. I checked a pregnancy test the next day and, to my surprise, it turned out to be positive. I was pregnant. I delivered a baby boy when I was twenty-six weeks pregnant, and we named him Samuel. His birth weight was only two pounds. But the God of the impossible kept him safe. He was discharged from the neonatal intensive care unit after seven weeks when he weighed five pounds. Jesus answered our prayers and turned our sorrow into joy. Praise the Lord. —V.K.

*****

Another story happened two and a half years ago. A mother brought her daughter up for prayer. The daughter was not able to conceive. We prayed for her and gave her a pair of anointed booties. Within a month, this young lady was pregnant, and she later delivered a healthy baby. About two years later, she gave birth to a set of twins. Yes, God wants to heal and place babies into people's waiting arms!

You might be wondering about the significance of the prayer booties. Several years ago, I started blessing couples who had problems getting pregnant by praying for them and giving them a pair of anointed booties. I instructed each of the husbands and wives to carry one of the booties in their pockets. Our ministry has given and sent these booties all over the world. All I ask for is a picture of the newborn baby wearing the booties. I can't even guess how many pictures of new miracle babies parents have sent into the office.

You might ask, "Were these just from everyday people? Or were these babies from mighty men and women of faith?" Both. Most of the miracle babies are from faithful believers who just wanted a child. A few of the couples are very well-known men and women of God who just needed an extra boost of anointing. God was faithful to bless each of them with a child.

If you desperately want the gift of a child, know that God is listening. Pray to him. Cry out to him. And believe in faith that he will answer you!

Pray this prayer:

Father, my heart's desire is to hold my own child in my arms. I know you have given others a miracle child. Since you aren't a respecter of persons, you can also bless me with a baby. I promise to give you all the honor and glory for this marvelous miracle and dedicate this child to you. Thank you, Father. In Jesus's name. Amen.

10

Miracle of Redemption

What in your life have you lost? Maybe it has been finances or time? God wants to redeem what the enemy has stolen from you. Everything and anything can be redeemed. This is the time and season when God can and will restore what the enemy stole from you. Stand and be ready to receive.

Everything in life is a form of exchange. If you want food, you have to grow it or pay for it. Years ago, people would often trade or exchange something they had for what they wanted or needed from someone else. Today, pawn shops will give money for something you wish to trade. Then, to get your belongings back, you have to redeem them with an exchange of money for the item.

Everything we do or want requires an exchange of some sort. Each day, God gives us twenty-four hours of time to use how we choose. We exchange our time daily for what we deem most important. Work, pleasure, people, rest—we trade our time for all of these. How much time do you spend with your family and friends? How much time do you exchange for work to make money to enrich your private time? How much time do you spend with God and his Word? Reading the Bible, you will learn that there are many exchanges necessary to redeem objects, including payment to God for sin or disobedience to his wishes and orders—some may call them his laws or the Ten Commandments.

How much is your relationship with God worth? What are you willing to "pay" to be in right standing with him? Would it surprise you to know someone miraculously paid your bill already? That's right. All you must do is accept that precious, free gift and follow the giver. Jesus has paid your redemption from sin forever. You are redeemed!

The Great Gift of Redemption

Why is redemption a miracle? Because Jesus Christ gave his life as a ransom or redemption for the sins of everyone who simply believes in him. That is a miracle! You don't have to pay anyone anything. You just have to accept Jesus and believe in him. It is such a simple principle. Many cannot comprehend that the blood of Jesus paid the total price for our salvation, our redemption once and for all eternity. Take a moment to reflect on these scriptures that reveal the miracle of redemption.

- A soul's redemption is too costly and precious for anyone to pay with earthly wealth. The price to pay is never enough to purchase eternal life for even one, to keep them out of hell. (Psalm 49:8–9 TPT)

- They forgot his great love, how he took them by his hand, and with redemption's kiss he delivered them from their enemies. (Psalm 78:42 TPT)

- As far as the east is from the west, so far has He removed our transgressions from us. (Psalm 103:12 NKJV)

- Since we are now joined to Christ, we have been given the treasures of redemption by his blood—the total cancellation of our sins—all because of the cascading riches of his grace. (Ephesians 1:7 TPT)

- In the Son all our sins are canceled and we have the release of redemption through his very blood. (Colossians 1:14 TPT)

- He appears to us as a mighty Savior, a trumpet of redemption from the house of David, his servant. (Luke 1:69 TPT)

- While Simeon was prophesying over Mary and Joseph and the baby, Anna walked up to them and burst forth with a great chorus of praise to God for the child. And from that day forward she told everyone in Jerusalem who was waiting for their redemption that the anticipated Messiah had come! (Luke 2:38 TPT)

- It is not from man that we draw our life but from God as we are being joined to Jesus, the Anointed One. And now he is our God-given wisdom, our virtue, our holiness, and our redemption. (1 Corinthians 1:30 TPT)

- Since a great price was paid for your redemption, stop having the mind-set of a slave. (1 Corinthians 7:23 TPT)

- He is given to us like an engagement ring is given to a bride, as the first installment of what's coming! He is our hope-promise of a future inheritance which seals us until we have all of redemption's promises and experience complete freedom—all for the supreme glory and honor of God! (Ephesians 1:14 TPT)

The Miracle of Redemption Today

My mother freely described herself as a "wild sinner," as she told off-color stories, smoked five packs of cigarettes a day, and drank alcohol freely. At age forty-nine, God got hold of her and changed her heart. She then became a "wild Christian" as she shared her salvation story with everyone and anyone she met. To say her life was changed is putting it mildly. She left her very successful printing business and started traveling to spread Jesus's Word across the country. Shortly after that, she met my dad and married him. Together, they spent the rest of their lives ministering healing, writing books, making videos, and, in general, serving God with their every breath. God used them to change the world!

Can you understand what God did? Can you fathom Jesus giving his life and shedding his precious blood for your redemption? It truly is a mental shift from poverty thinking to kingdom thinking. You don't have to fight every day to just survive. You don't have to have all the answers for every situation. Walk into God's kingdom through salvation and hold your head up high. God wants to bless you! You are a King's kid!

Pray this prayer:

Father, you gave your children such a precious, valuable gift in your Son, Jesus Christ. He loved us so much to actually open the door to redemption for us. Through his selfless gift, he paid the price for our mistakes, and we can now stand blameless in your presence. Thank you, in the blessed name of Jesus. Amen.

11

Miracle of a Renewed Mind

Just like redemption is a miracle, so is having a renewed mind—a mind cleansed of the lies from the enemy. When Jesus Christ renews your mind, you are essentially reprogrammed with his Spirit, which is available to call on anytime of day or night. With Christ in your life, your eyes open to his truth. Your opinions line up with God's thoughts, and your actions can follow his plans and desires. You might have heard the phrase *having the mind of Christ*. My mother wrote a book many years ago titled *Possessing the Mind of Christ*. In it, she talks about how transforming it is to have the mind of Christ, where his thoughts are our thoughts and his desires become our desires.

Some people who feel hurt, sick, depressed, or hopeless often blame God for their situations. God is the giver of good gifts, not those of pain and agony. The enemy pours his destruction over too many and then whispers, *If your God loved you, why would he do this to you?*

Do you want to stay stuck, or do you want to think God's thoughts and speak his words? Granted, you always have a choice because God gives everyone free choice. You can go back to your bondage of the world or walk in obedience into his love, joy, and peace. Read the following Scripture passages and then walk in faith, believing that he can—and will—give you the miracle of a renewed mind.

- Do not be conformed to this world, but be transformed by the renewing of your mind, that you may prove what is that good and acceptable and perfect will of God. (Romans 12:2 NKJV)

- Create in me a clean heart, O God, and renew a steadfast spirit within me.
  (Psalm 51:10 NKJV)

- Those who wait on the LORD shall renew their strength; they shall mount up with wings like eagles, they shall run and not be weary, they shall walk and not faint.
  (Isaiah 40:31 NKJV)

- Have put on the new man who is renewed in knowledge according to the image of Him who created him.
  (Colossians 3:10 NKJV)

- Not by works of righteousness which we have done, but according to His mercy He saved us, through the washing of regeneration and renewing of the Holy Spirit.
  (Titus 3:5 NKJV)

- Be renewed in the spirit of your mind.
  (Ephesians 4:23 NKJV)

- "Who has known the mind of the LORD that he may instruct Him?" But we have the mind of Christ.
  (1 Corinthians 2:16 NKJV)

Some people walk into one of our services in utter hopelessness with no plans for any type of a future. They tried to live with their pain and illness and failed. In the process of walking to the front of the room to request prayer, they suddenly realize they do have hope. With each hesitant step, the pain dissolves as they realize God does want to heal their mind and body.

Many people are almost unrecognizable after turning to God. They look younger and are happier than ever before. They walk in peace, confidence, and love.

At one service, a beautiful young lady came forward for prayer. She expressed her doubt that God would heal her, saying, "I don't feel worthy of getting healed." I prayed for her and assured her God loved her very much. She received healing, got ordained, and is now traveling with me as well as ministering on her own. She lost over fifty pounds during the first three months after getting healed. She has a beautiful smile on her face and knows without any doubt that God loves her more than she could ever imagine. Her friends and family often ask, "What happened to you?" which encourages her to share her story of redemption. God has even healed a family relationship!

Second Timothy says, "Do your best to present yourself to God as one approved, a worker who does not need to be ashamed and who correctly handles the word of truth" (2 Timothy 2:15 NIV). Ask and allow God to renew your mind so you can do what he has planned for your life. He will erase the pain of your past. He can wipe out bad memories. Rest in him, listen to him, and serve him. Drink from and feast on his Word, and he will clean and purify your heart, mind, and spirit. Enjoy this miracle in your life! Welcome it!

Pray this prayer:

Thank you, Jesus, for living within me and renewing my mind. Please teach me to listen and speak your words throughout every day and every situation. I want to think your thoughts and desire what you desire. In your name. Amen.

12

Miracle of Reconciliation

$\mathcal{H}$ave you ever had a fight or disagreement with someone that ended up destroying your relationship? Perhaps their words or actions upset you. Or you just couldn't see eye to eye on an issue. We've all had problems with people we didn't agree with or who didn't agree with us.

Situations happen between us and other people just as they happen between us and God. Something does not work out the way we want with a child, a parent, a friend, or a spouse, and the enemy uses that opportunity to try and pull us away from God with lies that interrupt God's perfect will for our lives.

One of the main reasons for divorce in the world today is irreconcilable differences, meaning the couple cannot agree or compromise in order to maintain the marriage. Usually, such disagreement causes estrangement, alienation, and total division. Some couples may say they become enemies. They firmly believe they can't reconcile their differences, and therefore, they must end the marriage.

What happens when people separate themselves from God because of their actions, beliefs, or total disobedience? Separation from our heavenly Father can cause extreme loneliness and helplessness. No one can take God to court to have a judge or jury offer their advice or verdict. Without reconciliation, restoration of harmony and peace is close to impossible. But God longs to restore our broken relationships—with friends, with spouses, and with himself. He is the ultimate healer, not just of our bodies and our minds, but also of our relationships.

Reconciled to God

God longs to reconcile you to himself first and foremost. When we choose to separate ourselves from God, it hurts him—just like it would any parent. Imagine that! The God of all creation wants to know you and love you. He wants to have a relationship with you and to restore the broken pieces of your heart and your life. Listen to God's instructions, his guidance, his Word.

- Not only that, but we also rejoice in God through our Lord Jesus Christ, through whom we have now received the reconciliation. (Romans 5:11 NKJV)

- God has made all things new, and reconciled us to himself, and given us the ministry of reconciling others to God. (2 Corinthians 5:18 TPT)

- In other words, it was through the Anointed One that God was shepherding the world, not even keeping records of their transgressions, and he has entrusted to us the ministry of opening the door of reconciliation to God. (2 Corinthians 5:19 TPT)

God can and will restore and heal every area of your life. Expect it. Even situations that you believe can never be repaired, God can and will do it. God knew man couldn't be perfect. In his omnipotence and wisdom, he gave us a way back to his throne, to his peace, and to his love, which has always been there waiting for us. He did not leave us. We chose to leave him. We made the choice to separate ourselves from him. But God is there, patiently waiting for us to shape up and ask for his help.

The Prodigal Son

Jesus brought great light to the subject of reconciliation when he told the story of the prodigal son. Anyone who has had problems with parents or children can relate to the pain in this father's heart and the loneliness and regret of the son when he realized his error. If it hasn't happened to you, I am sure you know someone who has lived through a similar situation. Let's look at this poignant story that illustrates God's great love for us and his desire to reconcile us to himself.

Jesus said, "Once there was a father with two sons. The younger son came to his father and said, 'Father, don't you think it's time to give me the share of your estate that belongs to me?' So the father went ahead and distributed among the two sons their inheritance. Shortly afterward, the younger son packed up all his belongings and traveled off to see the world. He journeyed to a far-off land where he soon wasted all he was given in a binge of extravagant and reckless living.

"With everything spent and nothing left, he grew hungry, for there was a severe famine in that land. So he begged a farmer in that country to hire him. The farmer hired him and sent him out to feed the pigs. The son was so famished, he was willing to even eat the slop given to the pigs, because no one would feed him a thing.

"Humiliated, the son finally realized what he was doing and he thought, 'There are many workers at my father's house who have all the food they want with plenty to spare. They lack nothing. Why am I here dying of hunger, feeding these pigs and eating their slop? I want to go back home to my father's house, and I'll say to him, "Father, I was wrong. I have sinned against you. I'll never be worthy to be called your son. Please, Father, just treat me like one of your employees.'"

"So the young son set off for home. From a long distance away, his father saw him coming, dressed as a beggar, and great compassion swelled up in his heart for his son who was returning home. So the father raced out to meet him. He swept him up in his arms, hugged him dearly, and kissed him over and over with tender love.

"Then the son said, 'Father, I was wrong. I have sinned against you. I could never deserve to be called your son. Just let me be—'

"The father interrupted and said, 'Son, you're home now!'

"Turning to his servants, the father said, 'Quick, bring me the best robe, my very own robe, and I will place it on his shoulders. Bring the ring, the seal of sonship, and I will put it on his finger. And bring out the best shoes you can find for my son. Let's prepare a great feast and celebrate. For this beloved son of mine was once dead, but now he's alive again. Once he was lost, but now he is found!' And everyone celebrated with overflowing joy.

"Now, the older son was out working in the field when his brother returned, and as he approached the house he heard the music of celebration and dancing. So he called over one of the servants and asked, 'What's going on?'

"The servant replied, 'It's your younger brother. He's returned home and your father is throwing a party to celebrate his homecoming.'

"The older son became angry and refused to go in and celebrate. So his father came out and pleaded with him, 'Come and enjoy the feast with us!'

"The son said, 'Father, listen! How many years have I been working like a slave for you, performing every duty you've asked as a faithful son? And I've never once disobeyed you. But you've never thrown a party for me because of my faithfulness. Never once have you even given me a goat that I could feast on and celebrate with my friends like he's doing now. But look at this son of yours! He comes back after wasting your wealth on prostitutes and reckless living, and here you are throwing a great feast to celebrate—for him!'

"The father said, 'My son, you are always with me by my side. Everything I have is yours to enjoy. It's only

right to celebrate like this and be overjoyed, because this brother of yours
was once dead and gone, but now he
is alive and back with us again. He
was lost but now he is found!'"
(Luke 15:11–32 TPT)

What a miracle that reunion and reconciliation was! Jesus used this story to show everyone just how much our heavenly Father loves us despite our foolish actions and sinful ways. God is waiting with great anticipation for each of us to run into his waiting arms. What a wonderful story of reconciliation and unconditional love!

Reconciliation in Action

During a meeting, I received a word of knowledge. Someone was experiencing stomach pain. A lady came forward to explain she had had abdominal pain for three months and had great difficulty eating anything. I asked her what had happened. She explained that her son had said, "I don't ever want to see you again!" As she heard his angry words, she felt like someone punched her in the stomach. I prayed for her abdomen to be healed and pain to go. I even told her, *he* would call *today*. She felt so good, she went to lunch with friends and actually ate. Before the end of the meal, she got a text from her son, "I miss you, Mom!" Her relationship with her son is now better than ever.

*****

Another lady had a son-in-law who didn't like her. She was very quiet about the problem and never said a word aloud. But under her breath, she repeated, *You will fall in love with me!* She seeded for the problem to disappear and laid him and the situation on the altar. Some time later, she discovered that someone in church hurt his family thirty-five years before. His family believed and often repeated, "You can't trust anyone in ministry!" This minister of the gospel prayed patiently and believed God for total reconciliation. When her daughter gave birth to their son, her son-in-law was given the privilege of naming the baby. He chose his mother-in-law's maiden name. They are totally reconciled, and he admits he now loves her.

*****

No two people can ever agree on every aspect of life. You may have heard the phrase "agree to disagree" to explain how we can respect someone else's opinion even while disagreeing with them, thereby maintaining the relationship rather than destroying it. To cooperate with others, we must have respect for other people and be willing to compromise. Stubborn, opinionated, and rigid people don't walk in peace or respect. When people experience separation, divorce, disagreement, or conflict, something specific must happen before unity can be restored.

The same concept applies to our relationship with God. He has given us his stand on every aspect of life in his written Word. Every man has an opinion from what the world has taught him. Which do you think is best? The world's opinion or God's? Who do you think is wisest? You or God? Who do you choose to follow? The world or God? Rejecting Jesus separates us from God and brings death. In Paul's letter to the people in Colossae, he wrote:

It was through what his Son did
that God cleared a path for everything
to come to him—all things in heaven
and on earth—for Christ's death on

the cross has made peace with God
for all by his blood. This includes you
who were once so far away from God.
You were his enemies and hated him
and were separated from him by your
evil thoughts and actions, yet now he
has brought you back as his friends.
He has done this through the death on
the cross of his own human body, and
now as a result Christ has brought you
into the very presence of God, and you
are standing there before him with
nothing left against you—nothing left
that he could even chide you for; the
only condition is that you fully believe
the Truth, standing in it steadfast and
firm, strong in the Lord, convinced
of the Good News that Jesus died for
you, and never shifting from trusting
him to save you. This is the wonderful
news that came to each of you and
is now spreading all over the world.
And I, Paul, have the joy of telling it to
others. (Colossians 1:20–24 TLB)

If you have separated yourself from your heavenly Father, please choose his Word and be reconciled to him. Return to his protection and provision. God is waiting for you with open arms.

And if you are in right standing with God, look to those around you. Witness to them and encourage them in their faith. Communicating God's love to others will draw them to God and your relationships will flourish. Your Christian family will multiply. Go back to the last line of Colossians 1:20–24 and place your own name in the last line: "And I, _____, have the joy of telling it to others."

Pray this prayer:

Father, I want to be reconciled to you. I want you to restore any part of me that isn't in agreement with you. Please search me and open my eyes to where I need healing. And as I walk this journey with others, help me to look to you when relationships are broken or damaged. Father, I want to walk in agreement with you. I realize there is power in that agreement. I know walking in your ways brings your peace, love, and joy. Thank you. In the precious name of Jesus. Amen.

13

Miracle of Righteousness

The word *righteous* is often misunderstood. Often we use it to describe a person who is good or who does good things. And while that can be true, the meaning of the word is actually much deeper than just acting good. A righteous man walks, talks, and lives in a position of righteousness with God.

The accurate interpretation or definition of *righteousness* is being in right standing with God. The world may consider a person to be *good*, but he or she may be far from being in correct standing with God. Outwardly doing something positive does not mean a heart is pure or good. Being in good standing with God opens the windows of heaven, allowing direct communication with him as well as permission to enter his presence. Think of it this way: if you wish to visit the supreme leader of any country, you must have the qualifications, meet the requirements, and have permission to enter his or her presence. Likewise, God's Word describes the rules and regulations necessary to enter his presence and talk with him. Being in right standing with the creator certainly is an honor and a privilege. Having permission to talk with God 24/7 is invaluable, and we should highly respect and treasure it.

Once you have attained righteousness in God's sight, why would you ever do or say anything to lose that status? God is our way to righteousness. He covers us with his perfection. He wants us to come into his presence to talk to him, praise him, and worship him. Since we are to become more and more like him, we should stay under his protection and loving arms. We truly can't earn or buy God's approval, but we can listen and obey.

Stay away from resentment and anything else that is not pure. Mimic God. Follow his guidelines. Maintain pure thoughts. Desire to be in right standing with him. Choose to have your relationship with God totally restored.

Keep in mind that righteousness is one of the blessings of salvation. Repent and accept his forgiveness. He is faithful and nothing that anyone has ever done will affect this precious gift of righteousness. No one has sinned so much that God will not restore righteousness to them.

But before we talk further about the wonderful gift of righteousness, let's first look at God's Word to see how he himself is righteous.

God's Righteousness

God's Word is full of scripture that tells of the righteousness of God. Read these verses and meditate on them. Praise and worship your heavenly Father in all his righteousness.

- The mercy of the LORD is from everlasting
  to everlasting on those who fear Him, and
  His righteousness to children's children,
  to such as keep His covenant, and to those
  who remember His commandments to do
  them. (Psalm 103:17–18 NKJV)

- He shall pray to God, and He will delight in him, He shall see His face with joy, for He restores to man His righteousness. (Job 33:26 NKJV)

- Lead me, O LORD, in Your righteousness because of my enemies; make Your way straight before my face. (Psalm 5:8 NKJV)

- The LORD shall judge the peoples; judge me, O LORD, according to my righteousness, and according to my integrity within me. (Psalm 7:8 NKJV)

- I will praise the LORD according to His righteousness, and will sing praise to the name of the LORD Most High. (Psalm 7:17 NKJV)

- The LORD is righteous, He loves righteousness; His countenance beholds the upright. (Psalm 11:7 NKJV)

- As for me, I will see Your face in righteousness; I shall be satisfied when I awake in Your likeness. (Psalm 17:15 NKJV)

- He restores my soul; He leads me in the paths of righteousness for His name's sake. (Psalm 23:3 NKJV)

- Commit your way to the LORD, trust also in Him, and He shall bring it to pass. He shall bring forth your righteousness as the light, and your justice as the noonday. Rest in the LORD, and wait patiently for Him. (Psalm 37:5–7 NKJV)

- The righteousness of the blameless will direct his way aright, but the wicked will fall by his own wickedness. The righteousness of the upright will deliver them, but the unfaithful will be caught by their lust. (Proverbs 11:5–6 NKJV)

- The work of righteousness will be peace, and the effect of righteousness, quietness and assurance forever.
(Isaiah 32:17 NKJV)

- With the heart one believes unto righteousness, and with the mouth confession is made unto salvation. (Romans 10:10 NKJV)

- Take up the whole armor of God, that you may be able to withstand in the evil day, and having done all, to stand. Stand therefore, having girded your waist with truth, having put on the breastplate of righteousness, and having shod your feet with the preparation of the gospel of peace.
(Ephesians 6:13–15 NKJV)

- This gospel unveils a continual revelation of God's righteousness—a perfect righteousness given to us when we believe. And it moves us from receiving life through faith, to the power of living by faith. This is what the Scripture means when it says:

"We are right with God through life-giving faith!" (Romans 1:17 TPT)

- Through his powerful declaration of acquittal, God freely gives away his righteousness. His gift of love and favor now cascades over us, all because Jesus, the Anointed One, has liberated us from the guilt, punishment, and power of sin! (Romans 3:24 TPT)

- When the season of tolerance came to an end, there was only one possible way for God to give away his righteousness and still be true to both his justice and his mercy—to offer up his own Son. So now, because we stand on the faithfulness of Jesus, God declares us righteous in his eyes! (Romans 3:26 TPT)

The Gracious Gift of God's Righteousness

It is totally amazing to me that God sees us one minute as sinners, black and lost to him. Then, when we accept Jesus as our Savior, it is like Jesus steps between us and God. Through the red blood of Jesus, God sees us white as snow. Black plus red equals white! Amazing! God sees our potential, not our past. He's such a good Father! Read these verses that show the gracious gift of God's righteousness:

- No one earns God's righteousness. It can only be transferred when we no longer rely on our own works, but believe in the one who powerfully declares the ungodly to be righteous in his eyes. It is faith that transfers God's righteousness into your account! (Romans 4:5 TPT)

- Our faith in Jesus transfers God's righteousness to us and he now declares us flawless in his eyes. This means we can now enjoy true and lasting peace with

God, all because of what our Lord Jesus,
the Anointed One, has done for us.
(Romans 5:1 TPT)

- I will greatly rejoice in the LORD, my soul
  shall be joyful in my God; for He has
  clothed me with the garments of salvation,
  He has covered me with the robe of righteousness, as a bridegroom decks himself
  with ornaments, and as a bride adorns
  herself with her jewels.
  (Isaiah 61:10 NKJV)

- Death once held us in its grip, and by the
  blunder of one man, death reigned as king
  over humanity. But now, how much more
  are we held in the grip of grace and continue reigning as kings in life, enjoying our
  regal freedom through the gift of perfect
  righteousness in the one and only Jesus,
  the Messiah! (Romans 5:17 TPT)

- Don't you realize that grace frees you to
  choose your own master? But choose

carefully, for you surrender yourself to become a servant—bound to the one you choose to obey. If you choose to love sin, it will become your master, and it will own you and reward you with death. But if you choose to love and obey God, he will lead you into perfect righteousness. (Romans 6:16 TPT)

- Having determined our destiny ahead of time, he called us to himself and transferred his perfect righteousness to everyone he called. And those who possess his perfect righteousness he co-glorified with his Son! (Romans 8:30 TPT)

- God made the only one who did not know sin to become sin for us, so that we who did not know righteousness might become the righteousness of God through our union with him. (2 Corinthians 5:21 TPT)

- We commend ourselves to you by our truthful teachings, by the power of God

working through us, and with the mighty weapons of righteousness—a sword in one hand and a shield in the other.
(2 Corinthians 6:7 TPT)

- We know full well that we don't receive God's perfect righteousness as a reward for keeping the law, but by the faith of Jesus, the Messiah! His faithfulness, not ours, has saved us, and we have received God's perfect righteousness. Now we know that God accepts no one by the keeping of religious laws! (Galatians 2:16 TPT)

- The Holy Spirit convinces us that we have received by faith the glorious righteousness of the Anointed One. (Galatians 5:5 TPT)

- You will be filled completely with the fruits of righteousness that are found in Jesus, the Anointed One—bringing great praise and glory to God! (Philippians 1:11 TPT)

- He himself carried our sins in his body on the cross so that we would be dead to sin and live for righteousness. Our instant healing flowed from his wounding. (1 Peter 2:24 TPT)

- If you know that he is righteous, you may be sure that everyone who lives in righteousness has been divinely fathered by him. (1 John 2:29 TPT)

Who has inspired me through the years? First and foremost, my parents, Charles and Frances Hunter. I was with them through the good and the bad. I watched them scale the mountains and refresh themselves in the valley of the King of kings, their Shepherd. They walked in such compassion and love towards everyone God brought across their path. I dearly loved my mom; however, she had to love me because she was my mom. Charles chose me as his daughter. He adopted me as a teenager and mentored me all the rest of his life. They both walked and talked a beautiful, inspirational Christian life. If I close my eyes, I can still hear their voices ringing through the atmosphere as they reach out to the hurting who need healing even today. Their books, CDs, and DVDs are available, and you can still enjoy countless hours of their teaching on YouTube.

Through the years, my dear friend and faithful mentor, Marilyn Hickey, has always been there for me. With Mom and Dad in heaven, Marilyn has become even more important to my life. She was always a good friend to Mom and Dad, and now she has become like a mom to me. She walks in such Christian integrity and love. Her guidance and words of wisdom have been invaluable to my life. In my lifetime, these are the people who most clearly exemplified lives filled with the fruits of righteousness and given to bring others to the saving power of the blood of Jesus.

Pray this prayer:

Father, thank you for the gift of your perfect righteousness—that even though I deserve death, you saved me. Help keep my heart pure. Give me strength to control my fleshly desires and to be discerning in what I place before my eyes. Help me to always walk and live in peace, not fear. Thank you. In Jesus's name. Amen.

14

Miracle of Obedience

Years ago, God directed a man named Mel Tari to take his group to a village in Indonesia to share the gospel. They walked for miles until they came upon a wide river swollen outside its banks from the rainy season. Their intended destination was a village on the other side, but they felt the wide expanse of water was blocking them from their assignment. There were no boats or bridges to use. They faced a seemingly impossible task.

Because God directed them to cross the raging river *now*, they chose to believe him and stepped forward to cross the water. The water came only up to their knees, and the entire group reached the other side safely.

Just behind them came another group of people who witnessed them wading through the water. Believing they could safely follow, they stepped into the river. This second group nearly drowned because the flowing water was actually very deep as well as dangerous. At that point, Mel's ministry team realized God had allowed them to walk on water. They reached their destination safely, preached the gospel, and raised a man from the dead.

Mel Tari documents this event well in his book, *Like a Mighty Wind*. You can also listen to his testimony on YouTube. He explains that years later, others came along and built a bridge in that area, so walking on water to cross that river was no longer necessary. In essence, man didn't need God's help crossing the water once they had built the bridge.

This miracle is not to be played with. God doesn't want you to be careless. If there is a bridge, use it. If there is no bridge and God tells you to cross, go for it. I have never walked on water; however, I have no doubt that if I truly needed to, I could! There is always power in obedience to God. He gives you what you need to obey him. If you don't obey his instructions, don't complain that you don't have what you need.

Peter's Obedience

After reading this story, it's impossible not to think of Peter stepping out of the boat to walk across the water toward Jesus.

> Now in the fourth watch of the night Jesus went to them, walking on the sea. And when the disciples saw Him walking on the sea, they were troubled, saying, "It is a ghost!" And they cried out for fear. But immediately Jesus spoke to them, saying, "Be of good cheer! It is I; do not be afraid." And Peter answered Him and said, "Lord, if it is You, command me to come to You on the water." So He said, "Come." And when Peter had come down out of the boat, he walked on the water to go to Jesus. But when

he saw that the wind was boisterous,
he was afraid; and beginning to sink
he cried out, saying, "Lord, save me!"
And immediately Jesus stretched out
His hand and caught him, and said to
him, "O you of little faith, why did you
doubt?" And when they got into the
boat, the wind ceased. Then those who
were in the boat came and worshiped
Him, saying, "Truly You are the Son of
God." (Matthew 14:25–33 NKJV)

Jesus gave Peter the order to "Come." And God made the sea hard enough so Peter could walk across the water. Peter knew Jesus well enough to step out in total faith, and Peter walked on the water until his human disbelief got in the way. Then he started to sink. If he would have kept his eyes on Jesus, he would have succeeded in reaching Jesus without getting soaked. Once Jesus grabbed him, Peter walked with Jesus back to the boat.

We, too, must keep our eyes on Jesus because he is our protector, Savior, brother, and best friend. Remember, as believers, we have the mind of Christ. Directions can come from him, our Father, or the Holy Spirit. Essentially, all instruction comes from God who wants only his best for each of us. We have to act, we have to choose, we have to exercise our spiritual faith and obey.

Once we make the choice to follow, it is God's responsibility to manage all the other details of our assignment. Staying in his presence brings all the other blessings he has prepared for us.

The Blessings of Obedience

Teaching obedience to children is so important. If children can't learn to obey their earthly parents, how can they obey an invisible God? Many don't even obey the laws of the land or teachers very well these days. Children must learn the benefits of obedience and the consequences of rebellious disobedience.

How often do you do good things for your obedient children? I love to reward obedience in people around me, and I believe God does the same for his children. Do you reward your children's disobedience? Of course not. God explains quite extensively what happens to the obedient and disobedient in Deuteronomy 28. One third of the chapter is about how God blesses our obedience (from prosperity to protection from our enemies) while two thirds explain the curses of disobedience to God's Word (from hunger and thirst to bodily harm and destruction). Read these instructions in Deuteronomy carefully and teach them to your children. Then enjoy the blessings of your miracle of obedience.

We recently bought a new home. The house is nearly a decade old, yet it looks brand new. The previous owners only used the home occasionally when they visited Houston, so we now get to enjoy a home that someone else built and barely lived in. This home, although just an earthly possession, has brought our family so much joy! We have a comfortable and safe place for our family to gather, a place where our grandkids can play and run, and a place where we can laugh and love each other. Talk about a blessing!

God also wants you to share the blessings he has chosen for you. This may mean giving to an established ministry or giving to the needy that surround us. When you bless others, God will in turn bless you in ways that you could never understand, think of, or imagine. If God tells you to give, do it joyfully and know that he will bless you accordingly.

Don't choose disobedience. Don't listen to the voice of the enemy. The penalty is not pleasant. Separation from God is not the path you want to go down. Choose life! Choose obedience and God's miraculous blessings!

Pray this prayer:

Father, show me the areas in my life where I am not following your instructions. Open my ears to hear you. Guide my life to stay on the path you designed for me. Thank you, Father, for all the miracles in my life—the ones I recognize and those I don't. You are a good Father and take care of me even when I don't realize it's you. I praise you. I love you. I worship you. In the name of Jesus. Amen.

15

My Challenge to You

In closing this book, I want to share a miracle story that once happened in my own life.

I was late leaving the house one morning and became increasingly irritated at the delay. I can't remember exactly what stalled me, but whatever it was, I just could not get everything together to get out of the house on time. Then, driving down the same route I took daily, suddenly I noticed heavier traffic than usual. When I finally reached the cause of the traffic, I saw three cars badly damaged and scattered about the road and about ten emergency vehicles blocking the highway. Creeping along through the crowded road, I quickly asked the policeman who was directing traffic what had happened. He explained that about fifteen minutes earlier, these cars had met with tragedy and destruction.

Thinking back on my morning, I realized that if I had gotten out of the house at the time I had planned to, my car could have been one of those involved in the collision. I may not have survived. The more I thought about it, I got goosebumps! With a big sigh of relief, I begged God's forgiveness for my complaining, and I started praising him for keeping me safe.

That scary situation changed the way I look at inconveniences. I no longer complain if something delays me or causes me to detour around traffic. Now I see this as a miracle from God. I know that God is directing my steps and will get me where I need to be right on time. And I trust that God will keep me safe.

Throughout this book, we have covered many miracles found in the Bible. And I have shared many stories of how God works miracles in our world today. My challenge to you as you finish reading is two-fold:

First, if you remember, earlier I asked you to write down the miracles you have experienced in your lifetime. Look back over that list. Continue adding to it. Meditate on it. Let God show you when he was working in your life.

As you start recognizing the miracles surrounding you, make note of them and then share them with me. I would love to hear from you. What has God done for you? Whether years ago or just this morning, let me know the newfound revelation that is playing out in front of your eyes.

Second, you can read about many more miracles in the Bible. As you study God's Word, jot down the miracles you find. Compare those events with things in your past. Does this help you better understand how God has worked miracles in your own life? Then share those experiences with your children and friends so they can also learn to recognize God's miracles.

Have fun and delight in God's wonderful, awesome world of miracles! From the beginning of time, God has shown himself to be a God of miracles. You are a walking miracle! And God continues to perform miracles all around you. Wait expectantly for the miracle you need today because

Miracles Happen!

Acknowledgments

A special thank you to Carlton Garborg, president of BroadStreet Publishing, for his encouragement in writing this book to bring greater attention to the fact that miracles happen still today.

A special thank you to Naida Johnson, RN, CWS, FCCWS, and ordained minister in the kingdom of God for her endless help in putting this book together—and for her input, editing, and wisdom in all areas of ministry.

About Joan Hunter

Joan Hunter is God's chosen miracle worker and anointed author stationed in Tomball, TX. Energized daily by the Holy Spirit, she is a dynamic teacher, compassionate pastor, anointed apostle, and faithful friend. Personal experiences with Joan relate to the many blessings attributed to her dedicated work and ministry. Miracles follow her as she shares God's revelations and wisdom directly from her heavenly Father to his children.

Joan has been a guest on numerous television and radio programs including Sid Roth's *It's Supernatural*, *Everlasting Love* with Patricia King, *Today with Marilyn* (Hickey) *and Sarah* and *My New Day* as well as many others. You can be blessed by her teachings through her numerous books, CDs, DVDs, live streaming, YouTube, and her powerful *Miracles Happen!* TV show. You can also find digital downloads of her teachings through Amazon.com and iTunes. Her current schedule of meetings and appearances is listed on her website http:/www.joanhunter.org.

Joan connects intimately with people from all walks of life with her genuine approach, candid delivery, and transparency. She follows the legacy of her parents, Charles and Frances Hunter, by reaching the lost, ministering healing, and teaching others how to duplicate the gifts God has blessed her with. Supernatural signs and wonders manifest during her healing schools, miracle services, and conferences in churches around the world. Testimonies of miracles come into JHM office daily. Many call her "Mama Joan" because of her compassion and love. As a prolific author, this is the twentieth book to come from her to reach people around the world. Many are available in other languages.

As president and founder of Hearts 4 Him and Joan Hunter Ministries, her vision is to equip believers to take the healing power of God beyond the four walls of the church to the four corners of the earth. Special conferences are held several times a year at her 4 Corners

Conference Center, including ordination/healing conferences twice a year.

Joan and her husband, Kelley, live in a northwest suburb of Houston, Texas. Together they have four daughters, four sons, three sons-in-law, and seven grandchildren. Joan is the daughter of the "Happy Hunters," Charles and Frances Hunter, whom she traveled and ministered with for some forty years.